Creative
RIBBONS
& ROSES

by Gail Rogers

Creative
HOUSE

CONTENTS

CONTENTS

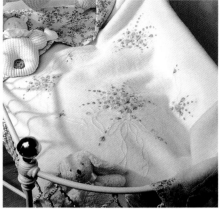

Published by Creative House
An imprint of Sally Milner Publishing Pty Ltd
PO Box 2104
BOWRAL   NSW   2576
AUSTRALIA

© Gail Rogers, 2003

National Library of Australia Cataloguing-in-
Publication data:

Rogers, Gail.
Creative ribbons and roses.

ISBN 1 877080 08 X.

1. Embroidery - Patterns. 2.
Ribbonwork - Patterns. I. Title.

746.44041

Printed in Hong Kong

EDITORIAL
Managing Editor: Judy Poulos
Photography: Richard Weinstein
Styling: Kathy Tripp
Illustrations: Lesley Griffith
DESIGN AND PRODUCTION
Production Director: Anna Maguire
Design: Jenny Nossal

Disclaimer
The information in this instruction book is
presented in good faith. However, no warranty
is given, nor results guaranteed, nor is free-
dom from any patent to be inferred. Since we
have no control over the use of information
contained in this book, the publisher and the
author disclaim liability for untoward results.

INTRODUCTION

This book is an extension of a love for embroidery that has been with me all my life. To embroider a garland of flowers or create a story with your needle is the same as an artist painting on canvas – it is creating in a third dimension with thread or ribbons.

I love the fabrics, threads, ribbons, wools, beads, buttons, charms, laces and braids available today. To be able to access all these wonderful mediums makes the art of embroidery very exciting. A thread, a piece of fabric or a flower in the garden all help to stimulate the creative juices and start you on the way to creating your own masterpiece.

This book is meant to be a guide only. My hope in writing it is to inspire and seduce you into creating your own designs. My wish for my students and fellow embroiderers is that it will foster their love of embroidery and a desire to achieve more.

I hope that you get as much pleasure from working the designs in the book as I did creating them. If you find the time to embroider one of the designs, or simply to relax and enjoy the beautiful pictures, I will have achieved what I set out to do.

Happy stitching!
Gail

ACKNOWLEDGMENTS

I would like to thank the following people: Judy Poulos, for making this book happen; Sandie Meldrum, for having faith in me; my ever-patient husband John and my children (Taryn, Simon, Bronwyn and Vincent) for allowing me my time and for their unselfish enthusiasm; Lynette Le Roy, Hilda Klass and my students from Thread Bearz, for the support and encouragement they have given me; Helen Kirkham, for proofreading and making suggestions; Shirley and Pam, for great Wednesday nights; and last, but not least, Jeff from Sterling Picture Framers, for framing my embroideries late into the night to meet my deadlines. To all of you 'Thank you'.

GETTING STARTED

MATERIALS

NEEDLES

It is important to choose the appropriate type and size of the needle you use to ensure a good result with your embroidery. It is also important that the needle suits your own style and technique. I like to work with very small needles – for example, a size 10 crewel needle for fine embroidery. The smaller the number (size) of the needle, the thicker the thread you can use. The larger the number of the needle, the finer the needle and the finer the thread and the fabric should be. The main thing to remember is to choose a needle which will create a hole in the fabric for the thread or ribbon to pass through with ease;

dragging the thread or ribbon through the fabric will cause damage.

Crewel needles are the standard hand-sewing needle, and are used for most forms of embroidery.

Chenille needles are large thick needles, which are generally used for silk ribbon and wool embroidery. They look like tapestry needles because they have a large eye and a thick shank, but the point is sharp.

Straw needles are long needles with a very small eye and are used for working bullion stitch. Because the shank of the needle is thicker than the eye, when it is threaded the needle slides easily through the bullion.

Tapestry needles are large, thick needles with a large eye and a blunt tip. They are used for tapestry and for weaving the thread or ribbon in spider roses. They are also used as a tool in loop stitch.

THREADS

There are so many threads on the market that the choice is vast. I have no particular favourites as I think they all have their place. I like to work with every medium – thread, ribbon, wool, beads and lace – to create the look I'm after. I also like to combine different threads in the same needle to create interesting textures.

When cutting thread, cut it no longer than the distance from your wrist to your elbow, as this stops the thread from becoming distressed with too much use. If the thread shows signs of wear, replace it.

Always separate stranded threads, then put them back together as this makes the thread pass through the fabric more easily.

EMBROIDERY HOOPS

I like to use a hoop at all times, as I find I get a better finish and have more control over the embroidery. For this reason, I would strongly recommend persevering with a hoop, even though some people find it difficult to use at first. The only time I don't use a hoop is when I am working on wool, because it distorts the fabric.

The choice of embroidery hoop will depend on the size of the design and the size of hoop you are most comfortable working with.

Binding the inner ring of the hoop with cotton tape will protect the fabric.

Keep the fabric tight in the hoop at all times and adjust it often. Never leave embroidery in the hoop if you are not working on it, as the fabric will become distorted.

Finally, using a hoop over work already completed requires great care so the embroidery is not flattened.

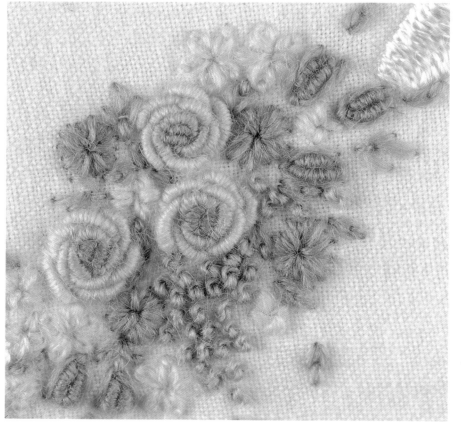

Close up of the Rose Garland Cushion on page 24

EMBROIDERY KIT

It is a good idea to have an embroidery kit or basket which includes the following: a small, sharp pair of embroidery scissors; a pair of dressmaking scissors; a pair of paper-cutting scissors; a tape measure; a water-soluble marker pen; a pencil; a pin cushion; some sharp pins; assorted needles; an awl; hoops of various sizes, and a thimble, if you use one. A small notepad to record hints or ideas is also a good idea.

SKILLS

TRACING THE DESIGN

I recommend water-soluble marker pens for tracing the designs onto fabric, because they are so easy to use, and when you wash or dampen the mark with water, it will disappear. I always use a water-soluble marker pen, as I can change the design at any time by simply touching it with a wet cotton bud.

When working on woollen fabric, begin by tracing the design onto a piece of tracing paper. Pin the tracing to the fabric and, using an awl or something similar, make holes in the pattern where the main flowers are. The hole should be big enough for the tip of the marker pen to go through, so you can mark a dot at each hole. Make sure the mark is clear. If it is not, place the pen tip in the hole again and twist it until a mark is visible.

For embroidering on silk or linen, there is no need to trace the design onto paper first – simply trace directly onto the fabric. If you cannot see through the fabric well enough to do this, tape the design to a window with the daylight coming through it. Tape the fabric over the top, then trace the design directly onto the fabric.

SILK RIBBON EMBROIDERY

Silk ribbon is used for embroidery in much the same way as regular embroidery threads.

Always use short lengths of ribbon, no longer than 30 cm (12 in). Any longer than this and the ribbon becomes distressed, starts to break up and the edges become fluffy.

To thread the ribbon and stop it from slipping out of the eye, pass the ribbon through the eye of the needle, then pass the needle through the end of the ribbon to secure it (Fig. 1).

Always treat silk ribbon with care and be gentle with it. Keep the ribbon loose when you are stitching, as this softness is the beauty of silk ribbon embroidery. The soft look is achieved with a gentle touch.

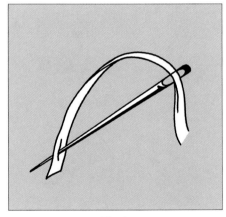

Fig. 1

LAUNDERING

Before laundering any piece of embroidery, it is imperative to remove all pen marks in cold water first.

In addition, special care is needed when laundering a finished piece of embroidery. Use only gentle soap solutions and dry the embroidery out of the sun.

To press the embroidery, place the piece face down on a clean, folded towel on the ironing board and press lightly on the back. Folded roses and some raised silk ribbon embroidery are better not pressed at all.

Always wash your hands before you start your embroidery. It is so easy to spoil a beautiful piece of work with dirty marks which can be difficult to remove later.

STITCH GUIDE

STEM STITCH

Stem stitch is used for embroidering stems of flowers and for outlining various shapes where an unbroken line is required. Keeping the thread under the needle, work from left to right. Take even and regular stitches, bringing the needle out halfway along the previous stitch, then make the next stitch (Fig. 1). Continue in this way until the line is completed (Fig. 2).

For whipped stem stitch, work a row of stem stitch, then work back along the row whipping under each one (Fig. 3). Take care not to stitch through the fabric when you do this. The whip stitch can be in the same colour as the stem stitch or in a different colour.

STRAIGHT STITCH

Straight stitch is a very simple stitch which can be worked at any length. Simply come up where you want to begin and go down where you want to end the stitch (Fig. 4). Straight stitch is very useful for working blades of grass (Fig. 5). A very loose straight stitch is called a puff stitch.

SATIN STITCH

Satin stitch is used to fill in an area with straight stitches that are worked very close together (Fig. 6). Work around the outline first, using split stitch or stem stitch, then fill in with satin stitch.

SPLIT STITCH

Often used for outlining, split stitch is worked in the same way as stem stitch, but instead of coming up beside the previous stitch, you come up through the previous stitch (Fig. 7).

LAZY DAISY STITCH

Lazy daisy stitch is often used to define petals on daisylike flowers. Take a small stitch from the inside of the flower, bring the thread around and under the tip of the needle to form a loop, then fasten the loop with a short or long straight stitch (Fig. 8). This is also called 'detached chain stitch'.

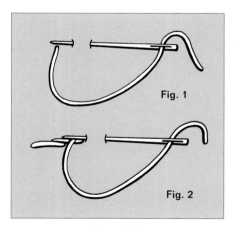

Stem stitch

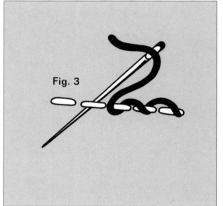

Whipped stem stitch

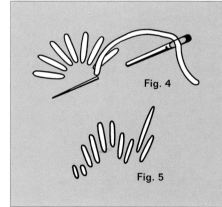

Straight stitch

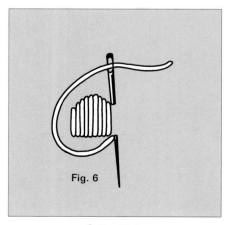

Satin stitch

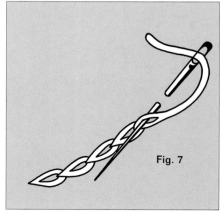

Split stitch

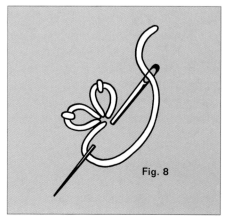

Lazy daisy stitch

FLY STITCH

Fly stitch is often used to embroider leaves. It is worked in the same way as lazy daisy stitch except that a Y shape is formed rather than a loop (Fig. 9). Many different effects can be achieved by altering the length of the stitches, by crossing them or by working them closer together.

FRENCH KNOT

French knots are among the most popular embroidery stitches. Begin by bringing the needle up where you want the knot to sit. Wrap the thread around the needle once, then take the needle back down as close as possible to the same point (Figs 10 and 11). With your free thumb, hold the loop right on the fabric while you gently pull the thread through to the back.

COLONIAL KNOT

Colonial knots are a little like French knots, but instead of simply wrapping the thread around the needle once, you wrap it in the shape of the figure eight (Fig. 12). Reinsert the needle as close as possible to the point where it emerged, and holding the knot close to the fabric with your free thumb, complete the stitch (Fig. 13).

BUTTONHOLE STITCH AND BLANKET STITCH

These stitches are often used to form a decorative edge. They are worked in the same way, except that buttonhole stitches are placed very close together. To make these stitches, bring the needle up and make a short stitch, keeping the thread under the tip of the needle, making a loop (Fig. 14).

BACK STITCH

Back stitch is a useful outlining stitch. Begin by bringing the needle out one stitch in front of where you wish to begin, then take a stitch back. Bring the needle up a little to the left of the last stitch, then take the needle back as before. Keep working in this way along the line (Fig. 15).

CHAIN STITCH

Begin by bringing the needle up through the fabric. Hold the thread with the thumb of your free hand and take the needle back into the same hole. Take a small stitch, keeping the thread under the needle, forming a loop. Take the needle back down through the loop and repeat, securing the previous loop (Fig. 16). Continue until the line of stitches is completed.

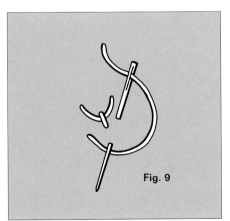

Fly stitch

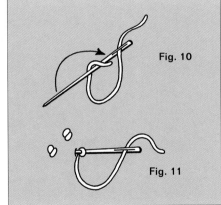

French knot

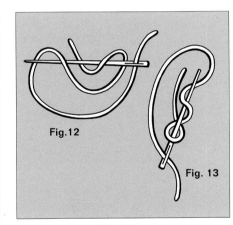

Colonial knot

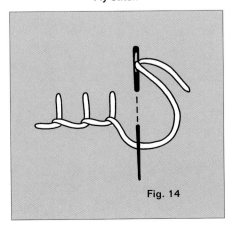

Buttonhole stitch and blanket stitch

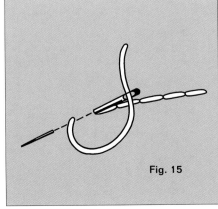

Back stitch

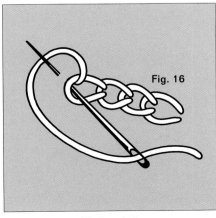

Chain stitch

BULLION STITCH

Bullion stitches are very popular stitches. They can be used alone or in groups to form roses and rose buds. To make a bullion stitch, begin with a small back stitch, then bring the needle back up, but do not pull it through (Fig. 17). Wrap the thread around the shank of the needle as many times as you require (Fig. 18). Holding the wrapped thread close to the fabric with the thumb of your free hand, gently pull the thread through, still holding the wraps close to the fabric with your free thumb. Reinsert the needle down at the beginning of the back stitch. The bullion will automatically twist around to be anchored at the beginning of the back stitch. Adjust it with your fingers so that it lies properly on the fabric. For the projects in this book, I will tell you how many wraps to make around the needle to create the rose.

PISTIL STITCH

This is like a straight stitch with a French knot on the end (Fig. 21). Bring the needle up while holding the fabric firmly with your free hand. Twist the thread around the needle from left to right (Fig. 19). Reinsert the needle a little way from where it emerged, holding the thread firmly with the thumb of your free hand (Fig. 20).

WOOL ROSE STITCH

This is the most popular way to form wool roses, using two shades of wool. Begin with five or six satin stitches in the darkest shade (Fig. 22). Work another five or six satin stitches over the first ones for a padded effect (Fig. 23). Using the lighter shade, bring the needle up halfway along the base of the square and take it down two-thirds

of the way up on the right-hand side. Work three more stitches alongside this one, each time finishing slightly higher until the last stitch is the same height as the square (Fig. 24). Turn your work and repeat this step three times until the rose is completed (Figs 25, 26 and 27).

FOLDED ROSE

This is a lovely way to make roses, using silk or organza ribbons. Begin by folding the ribbon edge over at an angle of 45 degrees, leaving a small overlap to hold onto, and roll the ribbon firmly to cover the folded edge (Fig. 28). Put a few stitches in to secure the centre. Continue making loose folds, reversing the ribbon at an angle of 45 degrees. As you roll it, place the top of the fold on the roll so the fold is vertical, forming a loose petal at the top (Fig. 29). Stitch to secure the petals at the base. Continue making petals in

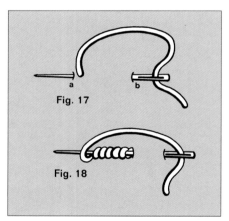

Fig. 17
Fig. 18

Bullion stitch

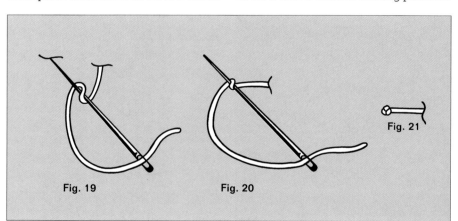

Fig. 19
Fig. 20
Fig. 21

Pistil stitch

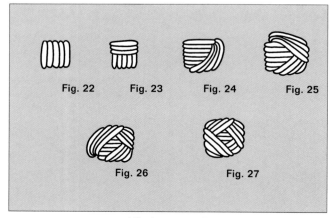

Fig. 22
Fig. 23
Fig. 24
Fig. 25
Fig. 26
Fig. 27

Wool rose stitch

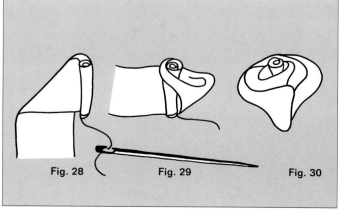

Fig. 28
Fig. 29
Fig. 30

Folded rose

this way. When you are pleased with the size and shape, cut and fold the ribbon so that all the raw edges are hidden, then stitch to secure (Fig. 30). Stitch the rose to the fabric with a matching sewing thread and stitch the petals down in a few places to achieve the desired effect (Fig. 31).

To create the buds, fold the ribbon two or three times over the roll and secure it with a few stitches. Make sure the cut ends are stitched under and are not visible.

SHADOW STITCH

Shadow stitch creates a very pretty, soft effect on a fine fabric. Begin by tracing the pattern onto the fabric. Working from right to left, work a small back stitch, then take the needle under the fabric, coming out slightly ahead of the next back stitch. Back stitch, then take the needle under the fabric up to the top, again slightly ahead of the next back stitch. Continue in this way until the area is filled (Fig. 32). For curved areas, adjust the length of the back stitches (longer on the outside of the curve and shorter on the inside).

RIBBON STITCH

This is a very effective way to stitch leaves, using silk ribbon. Bring the ribbon up through the fabric, lay it on top of the fabric, then pass the needle back through the ribbon (Fig. 33). Take care not to pull too tightly so that a soft curl forms at the end of the stitch.

LOOP STITCH

Loop stitch is worked with silk ribbon. Bring the ribbon up through the fabric where you want the stitch to sit, then take the needle back through, keeping the base of the ribbon flat on the fabric (Fig. 34). Slip a large tapestry needle through the loop to hold the loop in place until you make the next stitch (Fig. 35). Make the next stitch in the same way, using the large needle to hold the loop, as before.

WOVEN SPIDER ROSE STITCH

To make a spider rose, begin with a circle of five spokes, using an appropriate-coloured thread (Fig. 36). Using a tapestry needle, weave the ribbon or thread under and over the spokes until you have the desired fullness (Figs 37 and 38). Don't worry if the ribbon twists as you work – it will give the rose a more realistic appearance. To finish, take the ribbon through to the back and stitch in place with an oversew stitch. Finished rose (Fig. 39).

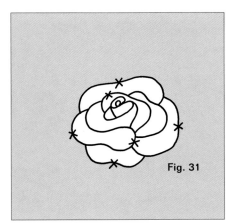

Fig. 31

Folded rose (finished)

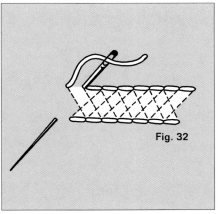

Fig. 32

Shadow stitch

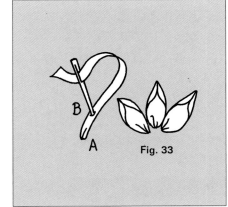

B
A
Fig. 33

Ribbon stitch

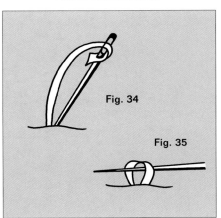

Fig. 34
Fig. 35

Loop stitch

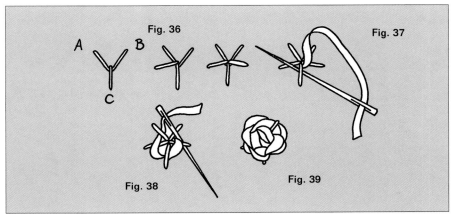

A   B
C
Fig. 36
Fig. 37
Fig. 38
Fig. 39

Woven spider rose stitch

TWISTED ROSE STITCH

Thread approximately 10 cm (4 in) of ribbon into the needle. Bring the ribbon up through the fabric where you wish the rose to be and twist it until the ribbon starts to buckle (Fig. 40). Reinsert the needle, close to where it emerged, but do not pull the ribbon through (Fig. 41). When the needle is just through the fabric, let the ribbon twist back on itself, forming the rose. You may need to stroke the ribbon to twist properly. Gently pull the ribbon to the back of the fabric and finish off (Fig. 42). With your fingers, arrange the petals in a pleasing shape and secure them in a few places with small stitches in a matching thread.

TRELLIS STITCH

First make a framework with a grid of long straight stitches. I weave the straight stitches under and over each other. Secure the points where the grid lines meet with small slanting or cross stitches, making sure they all face in the same direction (Fig. 43).

COUCHING STITCH

Couching is often used to secure very fragile or difficult threads to the fabric and is most commonly used with metallic threads. Lay the thread to be couched along the fabric, then stitch over it with small stitches (Fig. 44).

SURFACE STEM STITCH

This stitch is worked like stem stitch but it is worked through straight stitches sitting on the surface of the fabric. Work from the bottom of the design upwards, always keeping the thread under the point of the needle and keeping the tension even (Fig. 45).

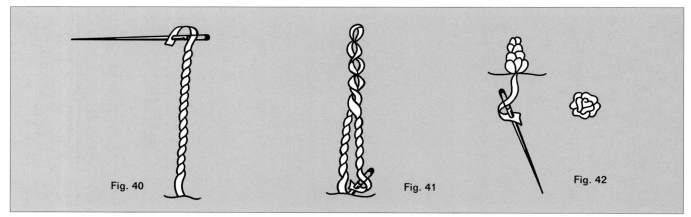

Twisted rose stitch

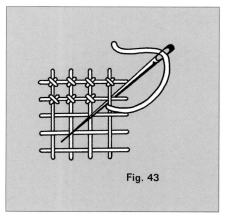

Trellis stitch

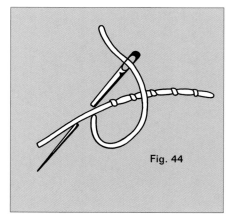

Couching stitch

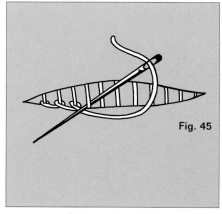

Surface stem stitch

ASSEMBLING A CUSHION

Beautiful embroidery deserves to be 'finished' with the same attention to detail as went into the embroidery itself. How disappointing to see a lovely piece of stitching spoiled by hasty and careless finishing. Following these few simple steps will ensure your cushion is a masterpiece.

CUTTING

1 Begin by cutting a 40 cm (16 in) wide strip across the full width of the fabric. When working on the straight grain of the fabric, I always draw a thread by making a small snip in the fabric and pulling a thread to the length I want to cut. This procedure is to ensure the fabric is square. Next, cut a 40 cm (16 in) square from this strip for the front of the cushion. This is the piece to be embroidered.

2 From the same strip of fabric, cut one piece 15 cm x 40 cm (6 in x 16 in) and one piece 32 cm x 40 cm (12½ in x 16 in) for the back of the cushion.

3 For the frill, cut three 20 cm (8 in) wide strips across the full width of the fabric.

TO MAKE THE FRILL

1 Join the strips end to end to form a circle (Fig. 1). Press the seams open. Fold the strip over double with the wrong sides facing and the raw edges matching. Press.

2 Fold the circle of fabric into quarters and mark the quarter points with pins (Fig. 2). This makes it easy to join the frill evenly to the cushion by lining up the four points marked with the corners of the cushion front.

3 On your sewing machine, gather the raw edges together with two rows of gathering stitches. Draw up the gathering threads to fit the cushion front.

Pin the frill to the right side of the cushion front, matching the quarter points with the corners and with the frill facing into the cushion centre (Fig. 3). Make sure that there are more gathers on the corners to make the frill sit neatly. Stitch the frill in place.

TO MAKE THE BACK OF THE CUSHION

1 To insert the zip, press under 3 cm (1¼ in) along a 40 cm (16 in) length of one back piece. Pin the zipper under the folded edges, close to the edge of the zipper. Sew it in place using the zipper foot on your sewing machine (Fig. 4).

2 Press under a 4 cm (1½ in) fold down the 40 cm (16 in) side of the other back piece. Pin the fold to the zipper, making sure it completely overlaps the zipper by 2 cm (¾ in), covering both the zipper and the previous seam line. Stitch the zipper in place (Fig. 5).

TO ASSEMBLE THE CUSHION

1 Place the back and front together with the right sides facing and with the zip towards the bottom of the cushion. Leave the zipper undone for turning the cushion right side out.

2 Pin the edges together, then stitch. Neaten the edges with zigzag stitching or overlock them. Turn the cushion right side out and place the cushion insert inside the cover.

TO MAKE A FRILL WITH LACE

You can attach a lace frill by pulling a thread along the top of the lace (most cotton laces will gather like this) or gather it up in the same way as for a fabric frill, then hand-stitch it in place. If you gather it up by machine, remove the gathering threads after you have attached the lace.

You can also attach lace to the frill by joining the lace and frill together, then gathering them as one piece of fabric. Attach them to the cushion front in the same way as the fabric frill.

I prefer to attach the lace to the cushion by hand as I think it gives a better result. Choose the method that best suits you.

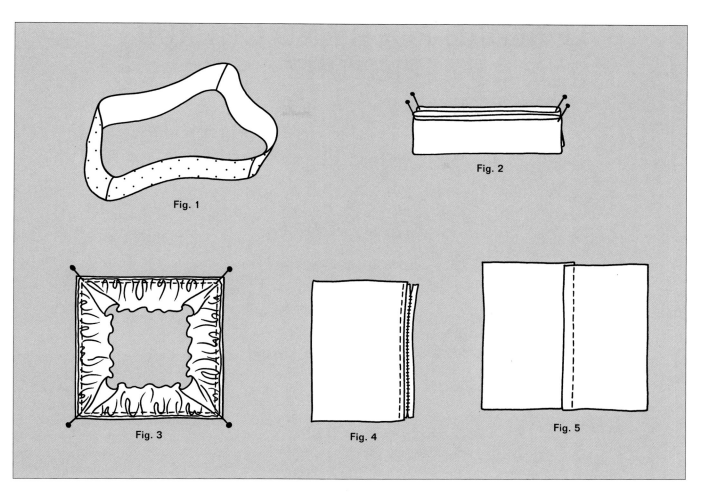

Fig. 1

Fig. 2

Fig. 3

Fig. 4

Fig. 5

FOLDED ROSE AND CHERUB PICTURE

This picture, incorporating delicate folded roses and silk ribbon embroidery, would look beautiful in a lounge or bedroom.

MATERIALS

40 cm (16 in) square of sage green dupion silk or moiré taffeta

Two 40 cm (16 in) squares of Pellon

4 cm (1½ in) 'antique' gold or ceramic (bread dough) cherub

Crewel needles, size 9

Chenille needles, sizes 18-20

Note: See page 6 for the appropriate needles to use with each type of thread.

23 cm (9 in) embroidery hoop

75 cm (30 in) of 15 mm (⅝ in) wide Makoubra Ribbon No. 4546, Dark Plum 92

1.5 m (1⅔ yd) of 15 mm (⅝ in) wide Makoubra Ribbon No. 4546, Mushroom 29

1 m (1⅛ yd) of 12 mm (½ in) wide Makoubra Ribbon No. 1505/12, Dark Green 16

1.5 m (1⅔ yd) of 7 mm (⁵⁄₁₆ in) wide silk ribbon, Mushroom 65

75 cm (30 in) of 7 mm (⁵⁄₁₆ in) wide silk ribbon, Plum 179

1 m (1⅛ yd) of 4 mm (³⁄₁₆ in) wide silk ribbon, Tan 57

75 cm (30 in) of 4 mm (³⁄₁₆ in) wide silk ribbon, Plum 179

50 cm (20 in) of 4 mm (³⁄₁₆ in) wide silk ribbon, Pale Plum 178

1.5 m (1⅔ yd) each of 4 mm (³⁄₁₆ in) wide silk ribbon: Pale Lavender Pink 83, Dark Green 72

1 skein each of Anchor Marlitt Rayon Thread: Tan 1037, Dark Green 1071

1 packet of Madeira Decora Rayon Embroidery Thread, Gold 1470

Ordinary sewing thread to match the ribbons

Water-soluble marker pen

PREPARATION

See the embroidery design on page 19.

STEP ONE

Fold the fabric in half horizontally and vertically to find the centre. Finger-press the folds.

STEP TWO

Place the embroidery design under the fabric for the front and trace the pattern with the marker pen. If you are unable to see through the fabric to trace the design, tape the design to a window with the daylight coming through it. Tape the fabric over the top, then trace the design onto the fabric.

STEP THREE

Baste one piece of the Pellon to the back of the fabric to be embroidered, then place it in the hoop, ready to commence embroidery.

Fig. 1

EMBROIDERY

STEP ONE

Satin stitch the bow, marked **A** on the design, in a single strand of Madeira Gold thread.

STEP TWO

Fold the roses, marked **B1** and **B2** on the design, following the instructions on page 10. Make one rose, using the Dark Plum ribbon and two using the 15 mm (⅝ in) wide Mushroom ribbon. Stitch the roses in place with the matching sewing thread.

STEP THREE

Stitch the leaves marked **C** on the design, in ribbon stitch, using the Makoubra Dark Green ribbon.

STEP FOUR

Stitch the fern, marked **D** on the design, in fly stitch, using a single strand of Marlitt Dark Green thread. Work a straight stitch for the tip of the fern.

Fig. 2

STEP FIVE

To work the briar roses, marked **E** on the design, work five loop stitches in the Mushroom silk ribbon. Place the stitches in a circle, leaving a small hole in the centre, about 3 mm ($^1/_8$ in) wide, for the French knots. Using the Tan silk ribbon, one French knot in the centre of each rose. Using a single strand of the Marlitt Tan thread, stitch three pistil stitches to each petal, making the centre stitch longer than the others (Fig. 1). Stitch French knots, in the Marlitt Tan, around the ribbon French knot.

STEP SIX

For the large padded buds, marked **F** on the design, work two straight stitches for the lower part, one on top of the other, in the 7 mm ($^5/_{16}$ in) wide Plum silk ribbon. For the upper part, stitch two straight stitches, one on top of the other, in the 7 mm ($^5/_{16}$ in) wide Mushroom silk ribbon. Using a single strand of the Marlitt Tan thread, stitch three pistil stitches on the upper petal, making the centre one longer than the others (Fig. 2).

STEP SEVEN

For the small padded buds, marked **G** on the design, work two straight stitches for the lower part, one on top of the other in the 4 mm ($^3/_{16}$ in) wide Plum silk ribbon. For the upper part, stitch two straight stitches, one on top of the other, in the 4 mm ($^3/_{16}$ in) wide Pale Lavender Pink silk ribbon. Using a single strand of the Marlitt Tan thread, stitch three pistil stitches on the upper petal, making the centre one longer than the others.

STEP EIGHT

For the small padded buds, marked **H** on the design, work two straight stitches for the lower part, one on top of the other in the 4 mm ($^3/_{16}$ in) wide Pale Plum silk ribbon. For the upper part, stitch two straight stitches, one on top of the other, in the Pale Lavender Pink silk ribbon. Using a single strand of the Marlitt Tan thread, stitch three pistil stitches on the upper petal, making the centre one longer than the others.

STEP NINE

Stitch the leaves marked **I** on the design on either side of the buds in ribbon stitch, using the 4 mm ($^3/_{16}$ in) Dark Green silk ribbon.

STEP TEN

Work French knots, marked **J** on the design, using the Pale Lavender Pink silk ribbon and a single strand of the Marlitt Tan thread mixed together in the same needle.

MAKING UP

Sew or glue the gold or ceramic cherub in place on the embroidered picture. I think it is best to have your picture professionally framed for a neat finish. I always put a second piece of Pellon at the back of my work before framing it, as this gives the embroidery more loft and the fabric sits flatter with no wrinkles.

Beautiful folded roses are a feature of this design

Embroidery Design

19

BRIAR ROSE POTPOURRI BAGS

The delicate silk ribbon embroidery, worked on silk, makes these potpourri bags a delightful gift.

Note: These two bags are worked in the same way; only the colours vary.

MATERIALS

For both bags

20 cm x 50 cm (8 in x 20 in) of ivory dupion silk
20 cm x 50 cm (8 in x 20 in) of cotton organza or Pellon
Crewel needles, size 9
Chenille needles, size 18
Cable needle, size 5
Note: See page 6 for the appropriate needles to use with each thread.
75 cm (30 in) of 25 mm (1 in) wide organza ribbon, Pale Pink, Blue Potpourri
1 g ($^1/_2$ tsp) of seed beads, Pale Pink
15 cm (6 in) embroidery hoop
Water-soluble marker pen
Tracing paper
Sharp pencil

For Bag 1

1.5 m ($1^2/_3$ yd) of 7 mm ($^5/_{16}$ in) wide silk ribbon, Cream 12
75 cm (30 in) each of 4 mm ($^3/_{16}$ in) wide silk ribbon: Cream 13, Lemon 14
1.5 m ($1^2/_3$ yd) each of 4 mm ($^3/_{16}$ in) wide silk ribbon: Green 31, Pale Blue 125
1 m ($1^1/_8$ yd) of 4 mm ($^3/_{16}$ in) wide silk ribbon, Very Pale Pink 83
DMC Stranded Cotton: Green 504, Pale Lemon 746

For Bag 2

1.5 m ($1^2/_3$ yd) of 7 mm ($^5/_{16}$ in) wide silk ribbon, Dusty Pink 163
75 cm (30 in) each of 4 mm ($^3/_{16}$ in) wide silk ribbon: Dusty Pink 163, Lemon 14
1.5 m ($1^2/_3$ yd) each of 4 mm ($^3/_{16}$ in) wide silk ribbon: Green 74, Pale Blue 125
1 m ($1^1/_8$ yd) of 4 mm ($^3/_{16}$ in) wide silk ribbon, Very Pale Pink 83
DMC Stranded Cotton, Dusty Pink 3688
Madeira Embroidery Silk, Green 1708

PREPARATION

See the embroidery design on page 22.

STEP ONE

Trace the embroidery design onto tracing paper. Fold the fabric in half lengthwise and fingerpress the fold. Centre the design under the fabric 6 cm ($2^1/_4$ in) from the fold line (Fig. 1).

STEP TWO

Trace the design onto the fabric with the marker pen. If you are unable to see through the fabric to trace the design, tape the design to a window with the daylight coming through it. Tape the fabric over the top, then trace the design onto the fabric.

STEP THREE

Baste the organza or Pellon to the back of the fabric, then place it in the hoop, ready to commence embroidery.

EMBROIDERY

FOR BAG 1

STEP ONE

For the briar rose, marked **A** on the design, work the petals in loop stitch, using the 7 mm ($^5/_{16}$ in) wide Cream silk ribbon. For the centre, work four French knots close together in Lemon silk ribbon. Using one strand of the Pale Lemon cotton, work thirty small French knots around the centre and three pistil stitches in each petal, making the centre one longer than the other two (Fig. 2).

STEP TWO

For the rosebud, marked **B** on the design, work two straight stitches, one on top of the other in 4 mm ($^3/_{16}$ in) wide Cream silk ribbon.

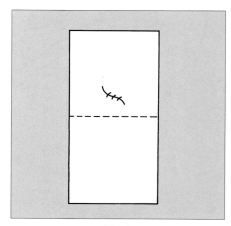

Fig. 1

Fig. 2

STEP THREE

For the leaves marked **C** on the design, using the Green silk ribbon, work twisted straight stitch twice on either side of the bud, making one of the stitches longer than the other. Make a straight stitch stem with a French knot at the base of the bud in the same colour.

STEP FOUR

For the pale pink blossom, marked **D** on the design, work small puffed stitches in Very Pale Pink silk ribbon. Stitch a cluster of seed beads in the centre of the flower.

STEP FIVE

For the forget-me-nots, marked **E** on the design, work five French knots in Pale Blue silk ribbon, leaving a space in the centre. For the centre, work a French knot in Lemon silk ribbon.

STEP SIX

For the leaves marked **F** on the design, work ribbon stitches in Green silk ribbon. For the leaves marked **G** on the design work fly stitches with a straight stitch tip in a single strand of Green cotton. For the leaves marked **H** on the design work lazy daisy stitches in a single strand of Green cotton.

FOR BAG 2

STEP ONE

For the briar rose, marked **A** on the design, work the petals in looped stitch, using the 7 mm ($^5/_{16}$ in) wide Dusty Pink silk ribbon. For the centre, work four French knots close together in Lemon silk ribbon. Using one strand of Dusty Pink cotton, work thirty small French knots around the centre and three pistil stitches in each petal, with the centre one longer than the others.

STEP TWO

For the rosebud, marked **B** on the design, work two straight stitches, one on top of the other in 4 mm ($^3/_{16}$ in) wide Dusty Pink silk ribbon.

STEP THREE

For the leaves marked **C** on the design, using the Green silk ribbon, work twisted straight stitch twice on either side of the bud, making one of the stitches longer than the other. Embroider a straight stitch stem, placing a French knot at the base of the bud in the same ribbon.

STEP FOUR

For the pale pink blossom, marked **D** on the design, work small puffed stitches in the Very Pale Pink silk ribbon. Stitch Pale Pink seed beads, close together in the centre.

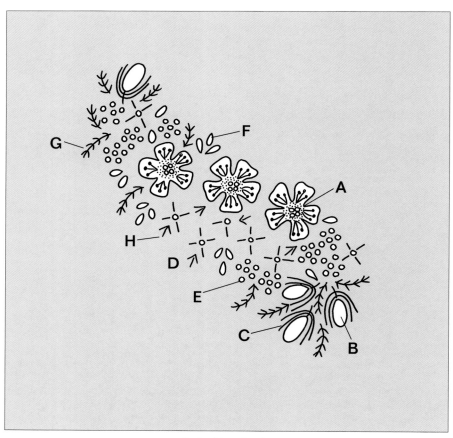

Embroidery Design

22

For the forget-me-nots, marked **E** on the design, work five French knots in Pale Blue silk ribbon closely in a circle, leaving a space in the centre. For the centre, work a French knot in Lemon silk ribbon.

For the leaves marked **F** on the design, work ribbon stitches in Green silk ribbon. For the leaves marked **G** on the design, work fly stitches with a straight stitch tip in a single strand of Green silk thread. For the leaves marked **H** on the design, work lazy daisy stitches in a single strand of Green silk thread.

MAKING UP

Sew up the side seams with very small French seams. Turn down 5 cm (2 in) at the top and hand-stitch the hem in place. Fill the bag with potpourri and tie a beautiful bow around the throat in organza ribbon.

Keep the ribbon soft for ribbon embroidery

ROSE GARLAND CUSHION

This cushion invokes just a touch of romance with its lovely soft colours and bow. The beautiful cotton lace completes the picture.

MATERIALS

1 m (1⅛ yd) of 115 cm (45 in) wide ivory homespun
40 cm (16 in) square of Pellon
30 cm (12 in) embroidery hoop
35 cm (14 in) zipper
3.6 m (4 yd) of 6 cm (2⅜ in) wide ivory cotton lace
Chenille needles, sizes 18–20
Crewel needles, size 9
Straw needles, size 8
Anchor Marlitt Rayon Thread: Ivory 1212, White 800
Appletons Crewel Wool: Dark Pink 753, Medium Pink 751, Pale Pink 877, Lavender Blue 461, Pale Lemon 872, Pale Green 351, Blue 561, Pale Purple 601
Ordinary sewing thread
Water-soluble marker pen
40 cm (16 in) cushion insert

PREPARATION

See the embroidery design on the Pull Out Pattern Sheet.

STEP ONE

Cut out the 40 cm (16 in) square cushion front from the homespun, as described in the instructions for assembling a cushion on page 14.

STEP TWO

Fold the fabric in half horizontally then vertically to find the centre. Finger-press the folds.

STEP THREE

Place the embroidery design under the fabric and trace the pattern with the marker pen. If you are unable to see through the fabric to trace the design, tape the design to a window with the daylight coming through it. Tape the fabric over the top, then trace the design onto the fabric.

STEP FOUR

Baste the Pellon onto the back of the fabric, then place it in the hoop, ready to commence embroidery.

EMBROIDERY

Note: For a close-up of the embroidery, see page 6.

STEP ONE

For the bow, marked **A** on the design, work satin stitches in two strands of Ivory thread.

STEP TWO

Work the roses, marked **B** on the design, in bullion stitch, using one strand of thread. For the centre, work two bullions of five wraps each in Dark Pink. Next, work three bullions of seven wraps each in Medium Pink around the centre. Finally, work six bullions of nine wraps around the outside in Pale Pink.

STEP THREE

Work the rosebuds, marked **C** on the design, in two bullions of seven wraps side by side, using one strand of Dark Pink. Fly stitch around the buds using one strand of Pale Green.

STEP FOUR

For the wisteria, marked **D** on the design, work 'bunches' of French knots using one strand of Lavender Blue.

STEP FIVE

For the daisies, marked **E** on the design, work five lazy daisy stitches for each daisy, using one strand of Pale Lemon.

STEP SIX

For the forget-me-nots, marked **F** on the design, work five French knots in one strand of Blue. Work a French knot in the centre in one strand of White.

STEP SEVEN

For the Easter daisy, marked **G** on the design, work straight stitches radiating out from the centre, using one strand of Pale Purple.

STEP EIGHT

For the periwinkle petals, marked **H** on the design, work three very small straight stitches going into the same hole, using one strand of Pale Pink. Make four petals for each periwinkle.

STEP NINE

Work leaves, scattered throughout the design, in lazy daisy stitch, straight stitch and fly stitch, using one strand of Pale Green.

MAKING UP

STEP ONE

Press the piece on a folded towel with the embroidery face down so as not to flatten it.

STEP TWO

Make up the cushion, following the instructions for assembling a cushion on page 14.

WOOL BROOCH PILLOW

A simple design in wool embroidery makes this brooch pillow elegant enough for any setting. All it needs are your favourite brooches to complete the picture.

MATERIALS

Two 20 cm (8 in) squares of white Onkaparinga wool blanketing
Small amount of polyester fibre fill
Chenille needles, sizes 18-24
Crewel needles, size 9
Note: See page 6 for the appropriate needles to use with each type of thread.
Anchor Tapestry Wool: Dark Pink 8368, Medium Pink 8366, Pale Pink 8362, Dark Green 9076
Paterna Persian Yarn: Pale Green A604, Lavender Blue A563, Yellow A745
DMC Perle 5 Cotton, Gold Yellow 676
Rajmahal Art Silk, Pale Yellow Green 421
Watercolours by Caron, Morning Mist
Ordinary sewing thread
Water-soluble marker pen
Tracing paper

PREPARATION

See the embroidery design on page 29.

Trace the embroidery design onto tracing paper. Place the tracing on top of one of the wool squares and pin it in place. Make holes in the pattern, big enough for the tip of the marker pen to go through, and with the marker pen, mark where you want to place the main flowers and leaves.

EMBROIDERY

STEP ONE

For the grub roses, marked **A** on the design, begin with two or three bullions of seven wraps side by side in Dark Pink for the centre (Fig. 1). Work between five and seven bullions of nine wraps in Medium Pink around the centre (Fig. 2). Finish with between eight and ten bullions of ten wraps in Pale Pink (Fig. 3).

STEP TWO

Work the leaves marked **B** on the design in fly stitch in Dark Green. Curl the first fly stitch over at the tip, then work the rest of the stitches quite close together (Fig. 4).

STEP THREE

For the buds, marked **C** on the design, begin with one bullion of seven wraps in Dark Pink for the centre. Next, work one bullion of seven wraps on either side of the centre in Medium Pink. For the outside, work one bullion of seven wraps on either side in Pale Pink.

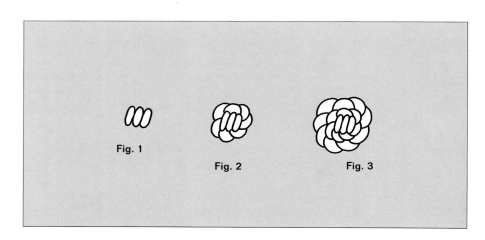

Fig. 1

Fig. 2

Fig. 3

Fig. 4

Fig. 5

STEP FOUR

For the leaves marked **D** on the design, work a fly stitch around the bud in Pale Green and add a small straight stitch from the base of the bud to the base of the centre bullion (Fig. 5). Place a French knot in the same colour at the base of the bud. Scatter lazy daisy stitches throughout.

STEP FIVE

For the forget-me-nots, marked **E** on the design, work the outside petals in French knots in Lavender Blue. Work a French knot in the centre in Gold Yellow Perle cotton.

STEP SIX

Work the daisy petals, marked **F** on the design, in five lazy daisy stitches in Yellow. Work one half daisy with two petals and the other with three petals.

Highlight the tips of the petals with a fly stitch in Rajmahal Pale Yellow Green. Add a straight stitch on the inside of the petals in the same colour (Fig. 6).

MAKING UP

STEP ONE

Place the two pieces of fabric with the right sides together. Stitch around all four sides, leaving a 7 cm (2³/₄ in) opening for turning. Turn the pillow right side out, then stuff it firmly and evenly with the fibre fill, pushing the stuffing right into the corners. Slipstitch the opening closed.

STEP TWO

Stem stitch around the seam line in Morning Mist, using all three strands.

Fig. 6

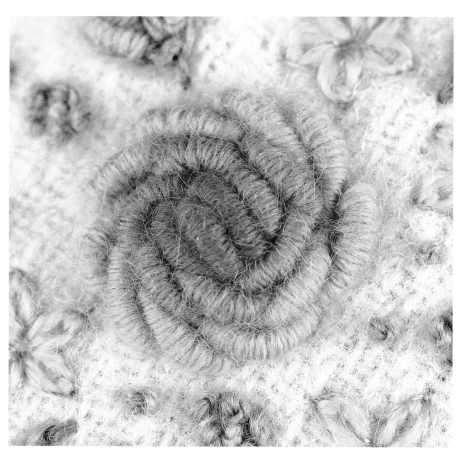

Place the bullions nestled close together

28

Embroidery Design

RIBBON AND ROSE LINGERIE BAG

This delicate lingerie bag invokes the charm of a past era. Creating this beautiful heirloom will give you a connection with this romantic time.

MATERIALS

75 cm x 90 cm (30 in x 36 in) of white voile

3.5 m (4 yd) of 4 cm (1¹/₂ in) wide cotton lace

1.6 m (1³/₄ yd) of white entredeux

Crewel needles, size 10

Straw needles, size 9

Note: See page 6 for the appropriate needles to use with each type of thread.

Ordinary sewing thread, White Madeira Embroidery Silk: Blue 1710, Pale Pink 0815, Medium Pink 0813, Dark Pink 0112, Green 1603

13 cm (5 in) embroidery hoop

Water-soluble marker pen

PREPARATION

See the embroidery design on the Pull Out Pattern Sheet.

STEP ONE

Cut two pieces of fabric, each 45 cm x 75 cm (18 in x 30 in). To ensure they are cut quite straight, pull a thread across the fabric as a guide for cutting.

STEP TWO

Place the embroidery design under the fabric for the front and trace the pattern with the marker pen, close to the bottom edge. If you are unable to see through the fabric to trace the design, tape the design to a window with the daylight coming through it. Tape the fabric over the top, then trace the design onto the fabric. Place the fabric to be embroidered in the hoop.

Note: Do not cut out the shape of the lingerie bag, until you have finished the embroidery and joined the two pieces.

EMBROIDERY

Note: All the embroidery is worked with a single strand of thread.

STEP ONE

Embroider the shadow-work bow in the Blue silk thread.

STEP TWO

For the centres of the grub roses, work two bullion stitches of five wraps each in Dark Pink. For the middle, work four bullions of seven wraps each in Medium Pink. For the outside, work six bullions of nine wraps each in Pale Pink.

STEP THREE

Work the leaves in lazy daisy stitch in Green. Work French knots in Pale Pink, scattered throughout the design.

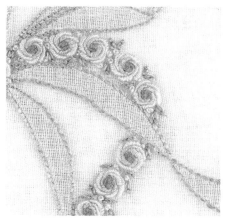

Only a single strand of thread is used for this delicate embroidery

MAKING UP

STEP ONE

Pin the two pieces of fabric together with the right sides facing. Trace the scalloped edge onto the fabric. Sew around the outside edge, leaving a small opening for turning. Cut out the scalloped edge, 6 mm (¹/₄ in) from the stitching. Clip into the seam allowance on the curves. Turn the piece right side out and hand-stitch the opening closed. Press carefully.

STEP TWO

Fold up 23 cm (9 in) on the end of the bag without the embroidery and pin it in place. Hand-stitch the sides closed with small oversew stitches.

STEP THREE

Trim the fabric from one side of the entredeux, very close to the edge. Pin the trimmed edge of the entredeux all the way around the edge of the bag. Hand-stitch the entredeux in place with small oversew stitches, going through each hole in the entredeux. Trim the other side of the entredeux.

STEP FOUR

Gather the lace by pulling a thread at the top of the lace. Pin the lace all the way around the edge of the bag, then hand-stitch it in place with small oversew stitches, again going through each hole of the entredeux.

GRUB ROSE CHRISTMAS TREE

This unusual Christmas tree has been densely embroidered with bullion roses for a very rich effect.

MATERIALS

30 cm (12 in) square of ivory homespun

30 cm (12 in) of Pellon

13 cm (5 in) embroidery hoop

Straw needles, size 8

Crewel needles, size 9

Note: See page 6 for the appropriate needles to use with each type of thread.

Madeira Embroidery Silk: Light Gold 2210, Medium Gold 2211, Dark Gold 2213, Red 0511, Maroon 0811, Dusty Pink 0812, Pale Dusty Pink 0403, Green 1314, Dark Green 1706, Dark Lavender 0806, Pale Lavender 0807, Blue 1710, Yellow 0114

Water-soluble marker pen

PREPARATION

See the embroidery design below.

STEP ONE

Fingerpress the square of homespun horizontally and vertically to find the centre of the fabric.

STEP TWO

Place the fabric over the embroidery design and trace the design with the marker pen. If you are unable to see through the fabric to trace the pattern, tape the design to a window with the daylight coming through it. Tape the fabric over the top, then trace the design onto the fabric.

STEP THREE

Baste the Pellon to the wrong side of the fabric, then place it in the hoop, ready to commence the embroidery.

EMBROIDERY

Note: All embroidery is worked using a single strand of thread.

STEP ONE

Outline the tree in French knots worked very close together in Green. Satin stitch the trunk in Green.

STEP TWO

For the red roses, work the centre with three bullions of ten to thirteen wraps in Red. For the outside, work ten to twelve bullions of fifteen to eighteen

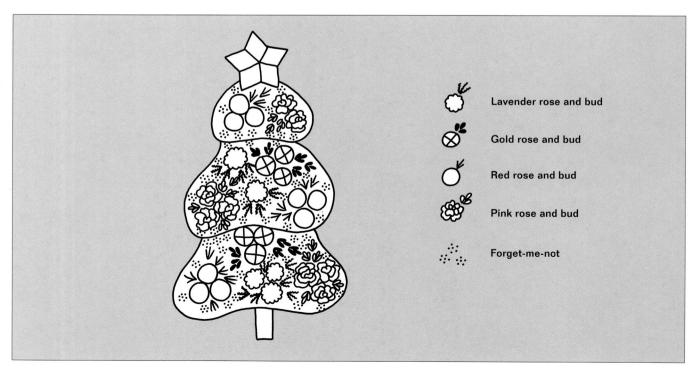

Embroidery Design

wraps in Maroon. For the buds, work three bullions of twelve wraps in Red. Embroider lazy daisy leaves in Green. Stitch two fly stitches around each bud, making one stitch longer than the other. This makes the bud look softer.

STEP THREE

For the pink roses, work the centres in three bullions of ten to thirteen wraps in Dusty Pink. For the outside, work ten to twelve bullions of fifteen to eighteen wraps in Pale Dusty Pink. For the buds, work three bullions of twelve wraps in Dusty Pink. Embroider lazy daisy leaves in Green. Stitch two fly stitches around each bud, making one stitch longer than the other. This makes the bud look softer.

STEP FOUR

For the lavender rose buds, work the centres in three bullions of ten to thirteen wraps in Dark Lavender. For the outside, work ten to twelve bullions of fifteen to eighteen wraps in Pale Lavender. For the buds, work three bullions of twelve wraps in Dark Lavender. Embroider lazy daisy leaves in Green. Stitch two fly stitches around each bud, making one stitch longer than the other.

STEP FIVE

For the gold rose buds, work the centres in three bullions of ten to thirteen wraps in Dark Gold. For the outside, work ten to twelve bullions

of fifteen to eighteen wraps in Light Gold. For the buds, work three bullions of twelve wraps in Dark Gold. Embroider lazy daisy leaves in Green. Stitch two fly stitches around each bud, making one stitch longer than the other.

STEP SIX

For the forget-me-nots, work the flowers in five French knots in Blue with a French knot centre in Yellow.

STEP SEVEN

Embroider the star in satin stitch in Medium Gold.

STEP EIGHT

Fill in any spaces with lazy daisy leaves and French knots in Dark Green. I like to make the embroidery so dense that you cannot see the background fabric.

MAKING UP

Frame the embroidery as you wish. I always use an extra piece of Pellon on the back of the embroidery as this gives it extra loft when it is framed.

Dense embroidery gives this piece a very rich look

GRUB ROSE CHRISTMAS BELL

This Christmas bell with its grub roses and antique-coloured silks will make a bold decorating statement.

MATERIALS

30 cm (12 in) square of ivory homespun
Two 30 cm (12 in) squares of Pellon
13 cm (5 in) embroidery hoop
Straw needles, size 8
Crewel needles, size 9
Tapestry needles, size 22
Note: See page 6 for the appropriate needles to use with each type of thread.
Madeira Embroidery Silk: Dark Gold 2213, Red 0511, Maroon 0811, Dusty Pink 0812, Pale Dusty Pink 0403, Green 1314, Dark Green 1706, Dark Lavender 0806, Pale Lavender 0807, Blue 1710, Yellow 0114
Water-soluble marker pen

PREPARATION

See the embroidery design on page 36.

STEP ONE

Fingerpress the square of homespun in half, horizontally and vertically to find the centre of the fabric.

STEP TWO

Place the fabric over the embroidery design and trace the design with the marker pen. If you are unable to see through the fabric to trace the design, tape the design to a window with the daylight coming through it. Tape the fabric over the top, then trace the design onto the fabric.

STEP THREE

Baste one piece of Pellon to the wrong side of the fabric to be embroidered, then place it in the hoop, ready to commence embroidery.

EMBROIDERY

Note: All the embroidery is worked using a single strand of thread.

STEP ONE

Embroider the inside of the top of the bell in Dark Gold and trellis stitch. Outline the top of the bell in chain stitch in Dark Gold.

STEP TWO

Embroider the inside of the bottom of the bell in surface stem stitch in Dark Gold. Outline the bottom of the bell in stem stitch in Dark Gold.

STEP THREE

Work the bell clapper in padded satin stitch in Dark Gold.

STEP FOUR

Stitch the ribbon in Dark Green and surface stem stitch. Outline the ribbon in stem stitch in Dark Green.

This embroidery makes a feature of interesting textures

STEP FIVE

For the red roses, work three bullions of ten to thirteen wraps for the centres in Red. For the outside, work ten to twelve bullions of fifteen to eighteen wraps in Maroon. Work the red rose buds in three bullions of twelve wraps. Embroider the leaves in lazy daisy stitch in Green. Work two fly stitches around each bud in Green, making one stitch longer than the other. This makes the bud look softer.

STEP SIX

For the pink roses, work three bullions of ten to thirteen wraps for the centres in Dusty Pink. For the outside, work ten to twelve bullions of fifteen to eighteen wraps in Pale Dusty Pink. Work the rose buds in three bullions of twelve wraps in Dusty Pink. Embroider the leaves in lazy daisy stitch in Green. Work two fly stitches around each bud in Green, making one stitch longer than the other.

STEP SEVEN

For the lavender roses, work three bullions of ten to thirteen wraps for the centres in Dark Lavender. For the outside, work ten to twelve bullions of fifteen to eighteen wraps in Pale Lavender. For the buds, work three bullions of twelve wraps in Dark Lavender. Work the leaves in lazy daisy stitch in Green. Work two fly stitches around each bud in Green, making one longer than the other.

STEP EIGHT

For the forget-me-not flowers, work five French knots in Blue for each flower. Work a French knot in Yellow for each centre. Fill in the design with as many leaves and French knots in Green as you think look attractive. I like to make the embroidery so dense that you cannot see the background fabric at all.

MAKING UP

Frame the embroidery in whatever way pleases you. I always use an extra piece of Pellon on the back of the embroidery as this gives it extra loft when the embroidery is framed and prevents wrinkles from forming.

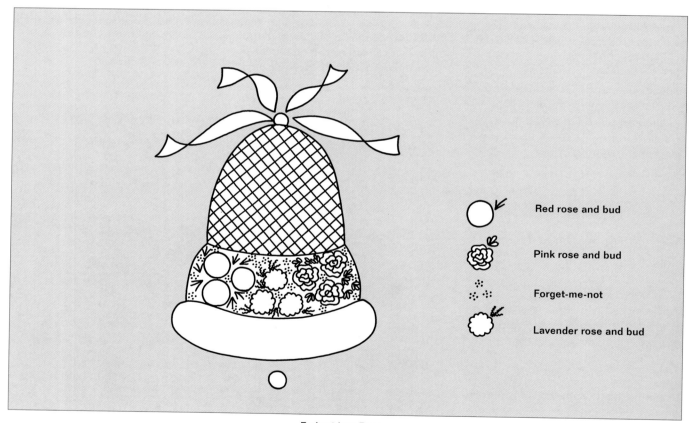

Red rose and bud

Pink rose and bud

Forget-me-not

Lavender rose and bud

Embroidery Design

PEARL HEARTS CUSHION

This dainty cushion with its soft colours and pearls could also be used
as a ring cushion, with the initials embroidered in the hearts.

MATERIALS

25 cm x 60 cm (10 in x 24 in) of fine
   ivory silk fabric
25 cm x 60 cm (10 in x 24 in) of
   Pellon
2.5 m (2³/₄ yd) of 5 cm (2 in) wide
   ivory cotton lace
Crewel needles, size 10
Straw needles, size 9
13 cm (5 in) embroidery hoop
3 g (1¹/₂ tsp) of small pearls, size 12
Waterlilies by Caron, Morning Mist
Au Ver a Soie Silk Threads: Green
   1743, Plum 4633, Medium Plum
   4631, Pale Plum 3332, Brut Cream
Ordinary sewing thread, Ivory
Fine pencil or water-soluble
   marker pen
Polyester fibre fill

PREPARATION

See the embroidery design on
page 40.

STEP ONE

Cut the Pellon and the silk fabric into
two pieces, each 25 cm x 30 cm (10 in
x 12 in). Set the Pellon pieces and one
piece of the silk aside.

STEP TWO

Place one piece of fabric over the
embroidery design and pin the two
together. Trace the pattern onto the
fabric with the fine pencil or the
marker pen. If you are unable to see
the pattern through the fabric, tape the
design to a window with the daylight
coming through it. Tape the fabric
over the top, then trace the design.

STEP THREE

Baste one piece of Pellon onto the
back of the fabric with the traced
design. Place the fabric with the
Pellon in the hoop, ready to commence the embroidery.

EMBROIDERY

Note: All the embroidery is worked in
a single strand of thread.

STEP ONE

For the roses, work two bullions of five
wraps for the centre, in Plum (Fig. 1).
Next, work five bullions of seven

wraps in Medium Plum around the
centre (Fig. 2). Finally, work seven
bullions of nine wraps in Pale Plum
around the outside (Fig. 3).

STEP TWO

For the rose buds, work two bullions of
five wraps for the centre in Plum. Next,
work two bullions of seven wraps in
Medium Plum. Finally, work two
bullions of nine wraps in Pale Plum.

STEP THREE

Work the leaves in lazy daisy stitch in
Green and the stems in stem stitch in
Green. Work a fly stitch around each
bud in Green (Fig. 4).

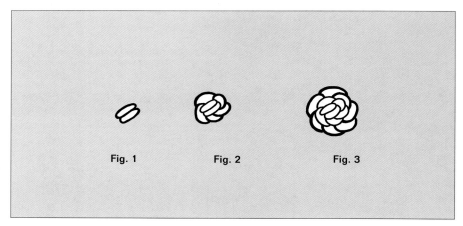

Fig. 1   Fig. 2   Fig. 3

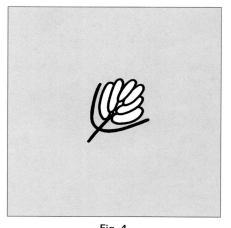

Fig. 4

Fig. 5

STEP FOUR

For the cream flowers, work a series of pistil stitches in a fan shape in Brut Cream (Fig. 5).

STEP FIVE

Stitch the pearls in place around the heart shapes, using the Ivory sewing thread. Place them close together.

MAKING UP

STEP ONE

Pin the other piece of Pellon to the back of the plain piece of silk. Place the embroidered piece and the plain piece together with the right sides facing. Sew the edges together,

through all thicknesses, leaving a small opening to turn the cushion right side out. Stuff with the fibre fill, then oversew the opening closed.

STEP TWO

Pull a thread along the top of the lace to gather it up. Pin the lace to the cushion, placing extra gathers in the corners. Hand-stitch the lace frill in place. Blanket stitch the ends of the lace together.

Embroidery Design

Silk grub roses and tiny pearls are a romantic combination

FOLDED ROSE CHRISTMAS WREATH

The colours of this wreath will look wonderful all year round, but they have all the richness of the Christmas season.

MATERIALS

40 cm (16 in) square of thick, cream silk fabric

40 cm (16 in) square of Pellon

Crewel needles, size 9

Chenille needles, sizes 18, 20 and 24

Tapestry needle, size 20

Note: See page 6 for the appropriate needles to use with each yarn.

25 cm (10 in) embroidery hoop

2 g (1 tsp) of Gold beads

1.5 m (1²/₃ yd) of 25 mm (1 in) wide wired ribbon, Old Gold

1.5 m (1²/₃ yd) of 7 mm (⁵/₁₆ in) wide silk ribbon, Bottle Green 21

2.5 m (2³/₄ yd) of 7 mm (⁵/₁₆ in) wide silk ribbon: Medium Dusty Pink 112, Dark Dusty Pink 159

2 m (2¹/₄ yd) each of 4 mm (³/₁₆ in) wide silk ribbon: Gold 54, Deep Purple 86, Dark Bottle Green 75, Dark Leaf Green 72, Khaki Green 143

5 m (5¹/₂ yd) of 4 mm (³/₁₆ in) wide silk ribbon, Pale Pink 157

5 m (5¹/₂ yd) of Makoubra Ribbon No. ES1505, Cherry Red 28

2 m (2¹/₄ yd) of Makoubra Ribbon No. ES1505, Grey 5

1.5 m (1²/₃ yd) of Makoubra Ribbon No. ES1505, Navy Blue 19, Dark Steel Grey 4

Watercolours by Caron, 1 skein of Meadow (Variegated Green/Pink)

Matsuhato Bunker Thread, 1 card of Gold 53

Anchor Marlitt Rayon Thread, Pink 1207

Ordinary sewing thread or stranded cotton to match the roses and bow

Water-soluble marker pen

PREPARATION

See the embroidery design on page 45.

STEP ONE

Place the fabric over the pattern and pin them together. Trace the pattern onto the fabric with the marker pen. If you are unable to see through the fabric to trace the design, tape the design to a window with the daylight coming through it. Tape the fabric over the top, then trace the design onto the fabric.

STEP TWO

Baste the Pellon to the back of the fabric, then place them in the hoop.

EMBROIDERY

STEP ONE

Tie a bow with the Old Gold wired ribbon and stitch it to the top of the wreath. Twist and turn the rest of the ribbon around the shape of the wreath, then stitch it in place. This will form the skeleton of the design.

STEP TWO

From the Cherry Red Makoubra ribbon, make five folded ribbon roses, marked **A** on the design. Stitch the roses in place around the design. Using the same ribbon, stitch two straight stitches, one on top of the other to form a padded bud, marked **B** on the design. Work a fly stitch around the bud in a single strand of Watercolours Meadow. Work another fly stitch, close to the first one, but a little longer to give it a feathery look. Work a straight stitch from the base of the bud and going down halfway up the bud (Fig. 1). Place some lazy daisy stitch leaves at the end of the bud.

STEP THREE

Make four two-toned folded roses, marked **C** on the design, using the 7 mm (⁵/₁₆ in) wide Medium Dusty Pink and Dark Dusty Pink ribbons. Place the two pink ribbons together and treat them as one. Stitch them in place.

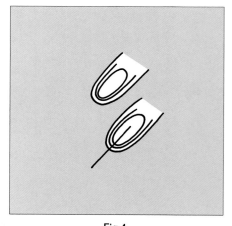

Fig 1

Fig 2

STEP FOUR

Using the Navy Blue Makoubra ribbon, make the large flowers, marked **D** on the design. Work five ribbon stitch petals, leaving a small space in the centre of each flower. Using the Gold silk ribbon, stitch five French knots in the centre. Using the Bottle Green silk ribbon, stitch ribbon-stitch leaves, marked **E** on the design, around the flowers (Fig. 2).

STEP FIVE

Work the purple daisy, marked **F** on the design, stitching eight or nine ribbon-stitch petals in Deep Purple silk ribbon (Fig. 3). For the centre, work a French knot in Khaki Green silk ribbon. Work the leaves in ribbon stitch and French knots in the Dark Leaf Green ribbon.

STEP SIX

Work the flowers, marked **H** on the design, using the Makoubra Dark Steel Grey ribbon. Group three ribbon-stitch petals together to form the flower. For the centre, work pistil stitch in the Gold Bunker Thread, coming up at the base of the petals and going down at the centre of the petal (Fig. 4).

STEP SEVEN

Work the forget-me-nots, marked **I** on the design, with five French knot petals in the Grey Makoubra ribbon for each flower. For the centres, work a French knot in Gold silk ribbon.

STEP EIGHT

Work the pale pink roses, marked **J** on the design, in spider stitch, using the Pale Pink silk ribbon.

STEP NINE

Work the bullion-flower clusters, marked **K** on the design, in the Watercolours Variegated Green/Pink thread. Work bullion stitches, using a single strand of thread.

STEP TEN

Work the leaves, marked **L** and **M** on the design, in lazy daisy stitch in Dark Bottle Green and Khaki Green silk ribbon. Scatter the leaves throughout the design, wherever you feel they are required.

STEP ELEVEN

Embroider French knots scattered throughout the design in four strands of Marlitt Pink thread. When all the embroidery is completed, stitch on the beads, arranged randomly throughout the design.

MAKING UP

Have the picture framed with a rich gold frame. When I have my pictures framed, I always place a second piece of Pellon on the back of the fabric as this gives the picture a nice loft and prevents wrinkles.

Richly coloured silk ribbons create an elegant appearance

Fig. 3

Fig. 4

44

Embroidery Design

ROSE MEDALLION

The medallion looks stunning on black silk, set in a gold box frame.

MATERIALS

20 cm (8 in) square of black dupion silk
20 cm (8 in) square of Pellon
10 cm (4 in) embroidery hoop
Crewel needle, size 10
Chenille needle, size 22
2 g (1 tsp) of seed beads, Metallic Light Plum
Ordinary sewing thread, Deep Pink Medallion
DMC Metallic Thread, Gold 282
3 m (3¼ yd) of 4 mm (³/₁₆ in) wide silk ribbon, Plum 158
1 m (1⅛ yd) of 2 mm (¹/₁₆ in) wide silk ribbon, Green 120
Anchor Marlitt Rayon Thread, Green 1030
White pencil

PREPARATION

See the embroidery design below.

STEP ONE

Fold the piece of black silk in half horizontally and vertically to find the centre. Fingerpress the folds.

STEP TWO

Centre the medallion on the fabric and draw around the inside with the pencil. Baste the Pellon to the back of the silk, then place the fabric in the hoop, ready to commence embroidery.

EMBROIDERY

STEP ONE

Embroider the twisted stitch roses first in the Plum silk ribbon. Sew the roses in place with the matching embroidery or sewing cotton.

STEP TWO

Embroider the straight stitch buds in the Plum silk ribbon. Work a fly stitch around the buds, in a single strand of the Green Marlitt thread, then work another fly stitch close to the first one but a little longer. Add a straight stitch to the centre of the bud.

STEP THREE

Work the leaves in ribbon stitch, using the Green silk ribbon.

STEP FOUR

Sew on the seed beads, using the Deep Pink thread. Sew scattered French knots throughout the design using the Gold thread.

MAKING UP

Place the medallion over the embroidery and sew it in place with the Gold thread. If you frame the embroidery yourself or have it framed professionally, place an additional scrap of wadding behind the medallion to raise the embroidery in the middle. I always put Pellon behind my embroidery to give the work extra loft.

Embroidery Design

Highlight the embroidery with tiny beads

NAIVE NATIVITY SCENE

This charming picture would look equally good as an
advent calender, framed, or as a small wall quilt to add to the
decorations each Christmas.

MATERIALS

50 cm (20 in) of 115 cm (45 in) wide
   seeded homespun
Two pieces of Pellon, each 50 cm x
   60 cm (20 in x 24 in)
30 cm (12 in) of 115 cm (45 in) wide
   fabric for the border
Small embroidery hoops
Novelty buttons for the angel and
   charms for the wise men
Beads: Gold, Pale Blue,
   Variegated Tan
Crewel needles, sizes 6-8
Chenille needles, sizes 18, 20, 24
Note: See page 6 for the appropriate
   needles to use with each type of
   thread.
DMC Perle 5 Cotton: White, Black
   310, Brick Red 221, Grey 644, Gold
   676, Pale Blue 794, Brown 839,
   Maroon Red 902, Dark Blue 930,
   Dark Green 935
Paterna Persian Yarn: Tan 443,
   Grey 147, Ivory 263, White 260
Appletons Crewel Wool: Blue Green
   156, Brown 184, Scarlet 505, Pale
   Gold 693, Flesh 701, Wine Red
   714, Pale Blue 742, Tan 763, Khaki
   953, Peacock Green 647, Black 998
DMC Stranded Embroidery Thread:
   Brown 3021, Black 301
DMC Metallic Thread: Gold 182,
   Silver 283
Madeira Glamour No. 8, 2458,
   Metallic Green
Watercolours by Caron: Teak,
   Desert Sage, Burnt Toast

Kreinik Metallics, Balger Blending
   Filament, Clear 032
Ordinary sewing thread to match
   the fabrics
Water-soluble marker pen
Tracing paper
Sharp pencil

PREPARATION

See the embroidery design on the Pull
Out Pattern Sheet.

STEP ONE

Cut the piece of fabric in half to make
two pieces, each 50 cm x 57 cm (20 in
x 22½ in). Fingerpress one piece
horizontally and vertically to find the
centre of the piece to be embroidered.

STEP TWO

Trace the embroidery design. Place
the fabric over the tracing, matching
the centres, and pin them together.
Trace the design onto the fabric with
the marker pen. If you are unable to
see the design through the fabric, tape
the design to a window with the daylight coming through it. Tape the fabric
over the top, then trace the design.

STEP THREE

Baste the Pellon to the back of the fabric, then place it in the hoop, ready to
commence the embroidery.

EMBROIDERY

STEP ONE

For Mary's dress, chain stitch the outline in Appletons Pale Blue, then stem
stitch the folds on the inside of the
dress in the same colour. Sew Pale
Blue beads between the folds to fill in
the dress. Chain stitch the outline of
the veil in the same colour. Fill in the
veil with alternating French knots
in Appletons Pale Blue and Pale Blue
Perle cotton. Satin stitch the shoes
in Brown Perle cotton. Stem stitch
the face and hands in Appletons
Flesh. Work French knots for the eyes
in Black Perle cotton. For the halo work
chain stitch around the outside and
straight stitch in the centre, using the
DMC Metallic Gold.

STEP TWO

Embroider the baby's blanket in trellis
stitch, using Maroon Red Perle cotton.
Stem stitch around the edge in the
same colour. For the straw, stem stitch
around the outside, then fill in with
straight stitches, using Appletons Pale
Gold. Stitch straight stitches in Gold
Perle cotton in between the Appletons
Pale Gold. Work the crib legs in chain
stitch, using Appletons Brown. Stem
stitch the halo in DMC Metallic
Gold and the baby's head, using
Appletons Flesh.

STEP THREE

For the mouse, satin stitch the body and the head, using two strands of DMC Brown. Straight stitch the tail in the same colour. Using the same colour again, work a lazy daisy stitch for the ear. Work a French knot in one strand of DMC Black for the eye.

STEP FOUR

For Joseph's coat, chain stitch around the outside in Appletons Blue Green. Fill in with fly stitch in Appletons Peacock Green. Satin stitch the cuffs, using Appletons Wine Red. Chain stitch the outline of the pants, using Appletons Brown. Satin stitch the shoes, using Black Perle cotton. Stem stitch the face and hands, using Appletons Flesh. Embroider the halo in blanket stitch, using DMC Metallic Gold, making the stitches uneven. Work French knots for the eyes in Black Perle cotton. For the beard, work French knots, stitched very close together, using Paterna Tan.

STEP FIVE

For the first Wise Man, embroider the coat outline in a single strand of Watercolours Teak and fill in with trellis stitch, using a single strand of the same colour. Work the trim on the coat and the hat in satin stitch in a single strand of Paterna Grey. Satin stitch the gloves, using Brown Perle cotton. For the beard, work French knots, very close together, in a single strand of Paterna Ivory. Blanket stitch the hat, using long and short stitches, in Gold Perle cotton and Gold metallic. Satin stitch the hat trim and cuffs in a single strand of Paterna Grey. Stem stitch the face, using Appletons Flesh. Work a French knot for the eye, using Black Perle cotton.

STEP SIX

For the second Wise Man, embroider the coat, using Brick Red Perle cotton, Appletons Scarlet and DMC Metallic Gold all in the needle together. Blanket stitch around the outside, then fill in with straight stitch. Blanket stitch to fill in the whole hat, using Madeira Metallic Green and Appletons Peacock Green together in the needle. For the hat trim, satin stitch in Grey Perle cotton. Blanket stitch around the outside of the beard, using Paterna Ivory. Stem stitch the face, using Appletons Flesh. Work a French knot for the eye, using Black Perle cotton.

STEP SEVEN

For the third Wise Man, embroider the coat, using Madeira Metallic Green and Appletons Peacock Green in the needle together. Work an uneven blanket stitch around the outside of the coat and fill in with straight stitch. Chain stitch the boots in Black Perle cotton. Satin stitch the coat trim and the gloves in Appletons Wine Red. Satin stitch the beard, using Paterna White. Using Dark Blue Perle cotton and DMC Metallic Silver together in the same needle, blanket stitch around the hat outline, then satin stitch the trim, using

Use different threads and stitches to create interesting textural effects

Paterna White. For the stick, chain stitch down one side then up the other side, using Brown Perle cotton. Stem stitch the face, using Appletons Flesh and work French knots for the eyes, using Black Perle cotton.

For the lamb's head and legs, stitch French knots very close together, using Black Perle cotton and Appletons Black, mixed together in the same needle. For the body, stitch French knots very close together, using White Perle cotton and Paterna White, together in the same needle. Stitch a French knot for each eye, using White Perle cotton and Paterna White, together in the same needle.

For the angel, chain stitch the outline of the dress, using Watercolours Desert Sage. For the wings, stitch straight stitches with a French knot on the end of each one, using DMC Metallic Gold and Silver together in the same needle. For the hair, work French knots, using Brown Perle

cotton. Stem stitch the face, using Appletons Flesh. Work French knots for the eyes in Black Perle cotton. Using Maroon Red Perle cotton and DMC Metallic Gold together in the same needle, stitch French knots for the beads and straight stitch the star. Sew the novelty buttons in place.

Stem stitch around the outside of the camel's body, using Appletons Khaki. Work a French knot in Black Perle cotton for the eye. Work the saddle in trellis stitch, using Watercolours Burnt Toast. Satin stitch the saddle trim, using Appletons Peacock Green. For the beads on the saddle, thread six Tan beads with one Gold bead on the end onto the needle and stitch them down with a straight stitch.

Stem stitch around the outside of the horse's body, using Appletons Tan. Work a French knot for the eye, using Black Perle cotton. Satin stitch the mane, using Appletons Pale Gold. For the tuft on the head, work oversew

stitches leaving the ends exposed, then cut them short and rub them till they are fluffy.

Chain stitch the tree, using Dark Green Perle cotton. Stem stitch the stable, using Watercolours Burnt Toast. Work French knots for the body of the spider and straight stitches for the spider's legs, using one strand of DMC Black cotton. Work the web in straight stitches, using Kreinik Clear. Chain stitch the outline of the star and straight stitch the star beams, using DMC Metallic Gold.

MAKING UP

To complete the wallhanging, baste the extra piece of fabric and Pellon to the back. Cut four 15 cm (6 in) wide strips from the border fabric. Sew them to the embroidered piece, right sides together and 6 cm (2¼ in) from the outside edge. Fold the border over to the back and hand-stitch it in place. Mitre the corners if you wish.

ROSE HEART WOOL CUSHION

Combine the softness of pure wool flannel with delicate folded ribbon roses to make this pretty cushion.

MATERIALS

35 cm (14 in) of 115 cm (45 in) wide cream wool flannel
35 cm (14 in) of Pellon
30 cm (12 in) cream zipper
1.5 m (1²/₃ yd) of cord edging
Ordinary sewing thread: Cream, Dusty Pink
Crewel needle, size 9
Chenille needles, sizes 18-24
Note: See page 6 for the appropriate needles to use with each type of thread.
25 cm (10 in) embroidery hoop
3.2 m (3½ yd) of 10 mm (³/₈ in) wide double-faced ribbon, Dusty Pink
2.8 m (3 yd) each of 6 mm (¹/₄ in) wide double-faced ribbon: Dusty Pink, Pale Cream
3.2 m (3½ yd) of 10 mm (³/₈ in) wide double-faced ribbon, Pale Cream
3 m (3¼ yd) of 7 mm (⁵/₁₆ in) wide silk ribbon, Green 31
DMC Perle 5 Cotton, Cream
Ordinary sewing thread to match the fabric and the double-faced ribbon
Water-soluble marker pen

PREPARATION

See the embroidery design on the Pull Out Pattern Sheet.

STEP ONE

Cut out a 35 cm (14 in) square of flannel for the cushion front. Fold the square of flannel in half horizontally and vertically to find the centre. Fingerpress the folds.

STEP TWO

Place the design under the front fabric and trace the pattern with the marker pen. If you have trouble seeing the design through the fabric, tape the design to a window with the daylight coming through it. Tape the fabric over the top, then trace the design.

STEP THREE

Baste the Pellon onto the back of the fabric with the tracing and place the fabric into the hoop, ready to commence the embroidery.

EMBROIDERY

STEP ONE

Satin stitch the appropriate parts of the heart in the Cream Perle cotton.

STEP TWO

Using the Dusty Pink and Pale Cream 10 mm (³/₈ in) wide double-faced ribbon, make ten large folded roses, marked **BP** (Pink) and **BC** (Cream), respectively, on the design. Stitch them in place with matching thread.

STEP THREE

Using the Dusty Pink and the Cream 6 mm (¹/₄ in) wide double-faced ribbon, make small folded roses and buds, marked **CP** (Pink) and **CC** (Cream), respectively, on the design.

Double-sided ribbon is perfect for these folded roses

Stitch them in place with matching sewing thread.

STEP FOUR

Using the Green silk ribbon, make the leaves, marked **D** on the design, in ribbon stitch. Start by bringing the ribbon up at the base of the bud and going down halfway up the bud. Work a ribbon stitch leaf on either side of the buds (Fig. 1). Place individual leaves throughout the design (Fig. 2).

STEP FIVE

Work French knots, marked **E** on the design, in Cream Perle cotton. Scatter them quite densely throughout.

STEP SIX

Using the 10 mm (³/₈ in) wide Pale Cream ribbon, fold a bow and stitch it in place on the design.

MAKING UP

STEP ONE

Pin the braid around the front of the cushion on the seam line, with the tape part of the braid towards the raw edge of the fabric. Snip the braid tape to ease it smoothly around the corners. Stitch the braid in place, using the zipper foot on the sewing machine to allow you to stitch close to the cord.

STEP TWO

Make up the cushion, following the general instructions for assembling a cushion on page 14, omitting the frill, which is replaced by the braid. Use the zipper foot for joining the front and back of the cushion.

Fig. 1

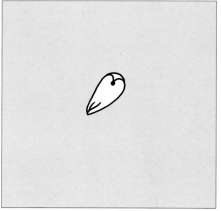

Fig. 2

HOT-WATER BOTTLE COVER

This personalised, wool-embroidered hot-water bottle cover will make you or a special friend warm and cosy all winter long.

MATERIALS

30 cm x 80 cm (12 in x 32 in) of Onkaparinga wool blanketing

30 cm (12 in) of 115 cm (45 in) wide fabric for the lining

1.5 m (1²/₃ yd) of 15 mm (⁵/₈ in) wide ribbon

Chenille needles, sizes 18-24

Crewel needles, sizes 8-9

Note: See page 6 for the appropriate needles to use with each type of thread.

Anchor Tapestry Wool: Dark Pink 8368, Medium Pink 8364, Pale Pink 9612, Very Pale Green 9074

Paterna Persian Yarn: Darker Green A603, Blue A514, Very Pale Pink A935

DMC Broder Medicis Wool, Green (fine) 8406

DMC Perle 5 Cotton, Grey Blue 928

Anchor Marlitt Rayon Thread, Yellow 1077

Au Ver a Soie Silk Thread, Yellow Green 3721

3 m (3¹/₄ yd) of 4 mm (³/₁₆ in) wide silk ribbon, White 3

1.5 m (1²/₃ yd) of 4 mm (³/₁₆ in) wide silk ribbon, Yellow 14

Rajmahal Art Silk, Leaf Green 421

Dewhurst 2144D Metallic Thread, Gold

Ordinary sewing thread

Water-soluble marker pen

Tracing paper

Sharp pencil

PREPARATION

See the embroidery design on the Pull Out Pattern Sheet.

Trace the embroidery design. Fold the fabric in half lengthwise and mark the fold line with a line of basting. Place the tracing on the 'front' section, 5 cm (2 in) up from the line of basting. Mark the pattern on the fabric by piercing holes in the tracing where the flowers and initials are placed, then use the marker pen to mark the positions.

EMBROIDERY

STEP ONE

Embroider the initial, marked **A** on the design, in chain stitch, using the Perle 5, Grey Blue.

STEP TWO

For the wool roses, marked **B** on the design, work the centre in wool rose stitch, using Dark Pink wool. Work the next round in wool rose stitch, using

Wool roses and silk ribbon daisies are a pretty combination

Medium Pink wool, then work stem stitches around the rose in Very Pale Pink wool. For the leaves marked **C** on the design, work scattered lazy daisy stitches in Very Pale Green wool.

STEP THREE

For the rosebuds, marked **D** on the design, work an open chain stitch with a straight stitch in the middle in Dark Pink wool. For the outside of the bud, work an open chain stitch in Medium Pink wool (Fig. 1).

STEP FOUR

For the small buds, marked **E** on the design, work French knots in Dark Pink wool.

STEP FIVE

Work the stems, marked **F** on the design, in stem stitch, using DMC Medicis Green.

STEP SIX

For the sepals, marked **G** on the design, work a fly stitch around the outside of the bud in DMC Medicis Green. Work two straight stitches at the top of the bud and a French knot at the base of the bud in the same thread (Fig. 2).

STEP SEVEN

For the highlights, marked **H** on the design, work three straight stitches on the buds, starting at the base and going down in the centre, using one strand of Rajmahal Leaf Green. Work a

fly stitch around the bud and a French knot at the base in the same colour (Fig. 2).

STEP EIGHT

For the large leaves, marked **I** on the design, curl a fly stitch over at the tip and stitch the rest of the fly stitches close together in one strand of Paterna Darker Green. Add straight stitch highlights using one strand of Rajmahal Leaf Green, stitched randomly over the shape of the leaf.

STEP NINE

For the forget-me-nots, marked **J** on the design, work French knots using one strand of Paterna Blue. For the centre, work a French knot in two strands of Marlitt Yellow.

STEP TEN

For the pink daisy, marked **K** on the design, work five lazy daisy stitch petals in one strand of Paterna Very Pale Pink. For the centre, work a French knot in one strand of Au Ver a Soie Silk Yellow Green and one strand of Gold metallic thread together in the same needle. Work highlights at the outside tips of the petals in fly stitch and straight stitch on the inside of the petals, using one strand of Au Ver a Soie Silk Yellow Green (Fig. 3).

STEP ELEVEN

For the silk ribbon daisy, marked **L** on the design, work lazy daisy stitch petals in White silk ribbon with a

French knot in Yellow silk ribbon for the centre. Stitch French knots in one strand of Au Ver a Soie Silk Yellow Green around the centre French knot.

MAKING UP

STEP ONE

Cut the lining fabric 30 cm x 92 cm (12 in x 36 in). Fold the fabric with the right sides together and stitch the side seams by hand or by machine.

STEP TWO

Fold the embroidered piece with the right sides together and sew the side seams. Turn it right side out.

STEP THREE

Place the lining inside the wool cover with the wrong sides facing. Baste or pin it in position. Turn 5 cm (2 in) of the lining out over the top of the wool. Turn under a 1 cm (³/₈ in) hem and hand-stitch it in place.

STEP FOUR

Stitch the centre of the length of 15 mm (⁵/₈ in) ribbon in place at the side seam where the lining and wool meet. Tie the ribbon in a pretty bow around the neck of the cover.

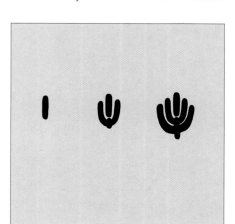

Fig. 1

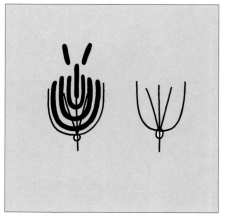

Fig. 2

Fig. 3

GRUB ROSE CHRISTMAS WREATH

The choice of colours and fine embroidery, make this little Christmas wreath very special.

MATERIALS

30 cm (12 in) square of ivory homespun
Two 30 cm (12 in) squares of Pellon
13 cm (5 in) embroidery hoop
Straw needles, size 8
Crewel needles, size 9
Note: See page 6 for the appropriate needles to use with each yarn.
Madeira Embroidery Silk: Gold 2210, Dark Gold 2213, Red 0511, Maroon 0811, Dusty Pink 0812, Green 1314, Dark Lavender 0806, Dark Green 1706, Blue 1710, Yellow 0114
Water-soluble marker pen

PREPARATION

See the embroidery design below.

STEP ONE

Fingerpress the fabric in half horizontally and vertically to find the centre.

STEP TWO

Place the fabric over the embroidery design and trace it with the marker pen. If you are unable to see through the fabric to trace the design, tape it to a window with the daylight coming through it. Tape the fabric over the top, then trace the design onto the fabric.

STEP THREE

Baste one piece of Pellon to the wrong side of the homespun, then place it in the hoop, ready to commence the embroidery.

EMBROIDERY

STEP ONE

Note: All the embroidery is worked using a single strand of thread.

For the bow, work French knots stitched very close together in Gold. For the shaded areas, work closely spaced French knots in Dark Gold.

Embroidery Design

Red rose

Pink rose bud

Lavender rose bud

Forget-me-not

STEP TWO

For the red roses, work three bullions of ten to thirteen wraps for the centres, in Red. For the outside, work ten to twelve bullions of fifteen to eighteen wraps in Maroon.

STEP THREE

For the pink rose buds, work three bullions of fifteen wraps each. Work the leaves in lazy daisy stitch in Green. Work two fly stitches around each bud in Green, making one stitch longer than the other – this makes the bud look softer.

STEP FOUR

For the lavender rose buds, work two bullions of twelve wraps in Dark Lavender. Work the leaves in lazy daisy stitch in Green. Work two fly stitches around each bud in Green, making one stitch longer than the other.

STEP FIVE

For the forget-me-not flowers, work five French knots in a circle, in Blue. Work a French knot in Yellow for each centre. Work the leaves in lazy daisy stitch and French knots in Dark Green and Green. Fill in the design with as many leaves in both shades of green as you think looks attractive. I like to make the embroidery on this piece so dense that you cannot see the background at all.

MAKING UP

Frame the embroidery yourself or have it professionally framed. I always use an extra piece of Pellon on the back of the embroidery as this gives it extra loft, when the embroidery is framed.

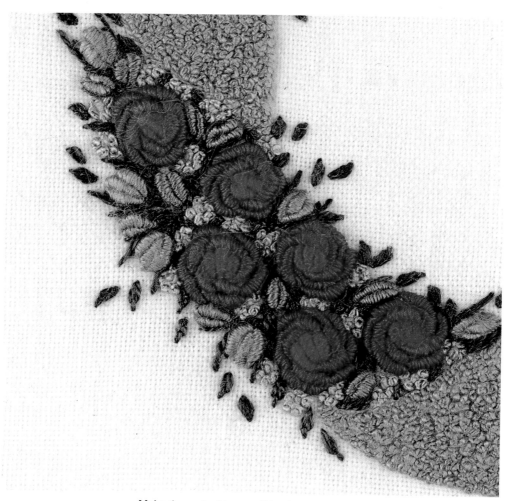

Make the embroidery on this piece very dense

WOOL BABY'S BLANKET

A gentle spray of spring flowers, gathered together with a ribbon bow,
makes this blanket perfect for a baby and is a pleasure to embroider.

MATERIALS

80 cm x 110 cm (31½ in x 43 in) of
   Onkaparinga wool blanketing
100 cm x 130 cm (39 in x 50 in) of
   printed fabric for the backing
3.6 m (4 yd) of 1 cm (³/₈ in) wide
   cream cotton lace
Chenille needles, sizes 18-24
Crewel needles, sizes 6 and 9
Note: Chenille needles are used for
   the wool embroidery, crewel
   needles size 6 are used for all
   Perle cotton and Watercolours
   embroidery, and crewel needles
   size 9 are used for sewing on the
   backing fabric and the lace.
Ordinary sewing thread to match
   the fabric
Paterna Persian Yarn: Medium Pink
   A924, Light Pink A491, Pale Laven-
   der D147, Bridal White A263,
   Lemon A704, Green A604
DMC Perle 5 Cotton: Very Pale
   Lemon 746, Pale Lavender Grey
   415, Gold 676, Cream 712
Watercolours by Caron, Peach
   Sherbet
Water-soluble marker pen
Tracing paper
Sharp pencil

PREPARATION

See the embroidery design on the Pull
Out Pattern Sheet.

STEP ONE

Run a large basting thread horizontally
and vertically on the wool fabric to
mark the centre.

STEP TWO

Trace the design from the pattern
sheet and centre it on the blanket.
Make holes in the pattern just big
enough for the tip of the marking
pen to go through, then mark dots on
the blanket where the flowers and
ribbon will be embroidered, using
the marker pen. For the ribbon, mark
dots on all the points and inter-
sections, then lift the pattern and draw
in the ribbon freehand, connecting
the dots.

EMBROIDERY

STEP ONE

Stitch the outline of the bow, marked
A on the design, in chain stitch in the
Very Pale Lemon cotton.

STEP TWO

For the wool rose, marked **B** on the
design, work the centre in wool rose
stitch in one strand of Medium Pink.
Embroider the outside in wool rose
stitch in one strand of Light Pink.

STEP THREE

For the buds, marked **C** on the design,
work the centre in three straight
stitches going in and out of the same
holes in one strand of Medium Pink.
For the outside, work three straight
stitches going in and out of the same
holes on one side of the bud and
crossing over at the base, in one strand
of Light Pink. Repeat for the other side
of the bud. Using one strand of Green,
work a fly stitch around each bud and
place a straight stitch in the centre of

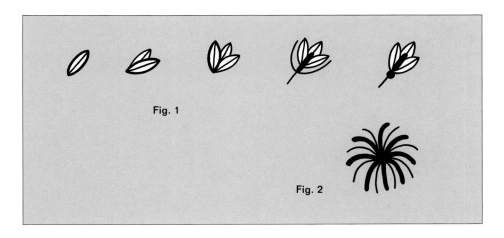

Fig. 1

Fig. 2

the bud coming up at the base and going down halfway up the bud. Finish with a French knot at the base of the bud in the same colour (Fig. 1).

STEP FOUR

Work the leaves, marked **D** on the design, in lazy daisy stitch in one strand of Green. Place a lazy daisy stitch at the tip of the bud and work groups of three lazy daisy stitches around the roses.

STEP FIVE

For the daisies, marked **E** on the design, work six or seven lazy daisy stitches for each flower in one strand of Lemon wool. Work a straight stitch in Gold cotton in the centre of each petal.

STEP SIX

For the lavender flowers, marked **F** on the design, work very loose straight stitches radiating out from the centre in Pale Lavender wool (Fig. 2). Keep the stitches raised above the surface of the work. Using Pale Lavender Grey cotton, place a raised straight stitch between each wool petal.

STEP SEVEN

For the forget-me-nots, marked **G** on the design, work five French knots in a single strand of Peach Sherbet. For the centre, work a French knot in Gold.

Keep the embroidery and the yarn colours soft for this piece

STEP EIGHT

Work French knots scattered randomly throughout the design, wherever you think they will look attractive, using Bridal White wool and Cream cotton together in the same needle.

MAKING UP

STEP ONE

Place the printed backing fabric face down. Place the embroidered wool, right side up, on top of the backing and pin it in place. Fold the corners at an angle of 45 degrees, then fold in the sides, turning under 5 cm (2 in) so you have a 5 cm (2 in) border of the backing showing on the front of the blanket (Fig. 3). Pin the border in place. Trim away any material showing on the corners so that you have a neat mitred edge. Slipstitch the border, taking care not to go through the backing.

STEP TWO

Pin the lace in place, facing in to the centre of the blanket, then hand-stitch it in place (Fig. 4).

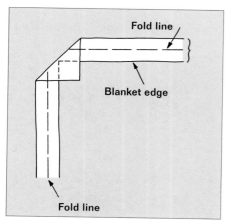

Fig. 3

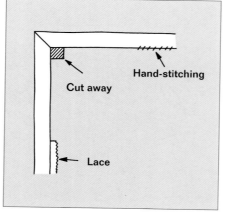

Fig. 4

NAIVE BAG

This bag is fun and quick to embroider with its bright colours and simple design.

MATERIALS

50 cm x 115 cm (20 in x 45 in) of Osnanberg or calico (natural seeded)

25 cm x 60 cm (10 in x 24 in) of Pellon or cotton wadding

Gold heart charm

Cotton Fields 4-ply Cotton Yarn: Cream 103, Tan 106

Crewel needles, size 6

DMC Perle 5 Cotton: Dark Blue 930, Dark Green 936, Pale Yellow 676, Pale Brown 840, Gold 977, Red 817, Medium Green 937, Teal Blue 924, Khaki Brown 644, Maroon 902, Lime Green 472, Yellow 742, Pale Brick 356

Appletons Crewel Wool: White 881, Tan 763

DMC Broder Medicis Wool, Pale Brown 8503

DMC Stranded Cotton, Black 310

Ordinary sewing thread to match the fabric

Water-soluble marker pen

15 cm (6 in) embroidery hoop

Tracing paper

Sharp pencil

4.5 cm (1³/₄ in) wide cardboard

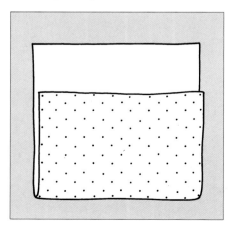

Fig. 1

PREPARATION

See the embroidery design on page 67.

STEP ONE

Cut two pieces of fabric, each 25 cm x 60 cm (10 in x 24 in). Fold one piece over as shown in figure 1. Fingerpress the fold.

STEP TWO

Trace the design and place it under the folded section, ensuring that the bottom of the design is 1.5 cm (⁵/₈ in) from the fold. Pin the design and fabric together, then trace the design onto the fabric with the marker pen. If you are unable to see the design through the fabric, tape the tracing to a window with daylight coming through it and tape the fabric over the top.

STEP THREE

Baste the Pellon to the back of the piece of fabric to be embroidered. Place it in the hoop, ready to commence embroidery.

EMBROIDERY

STEP ONE

For the lamb's body, work French knots very close together, using two strands of White and one strand of Tan wool. Stem stitch the legs in Pale Brown Perle cotton. Straight stitch the ears and nose and work a colonial knot for the eye in the same colour. Work colonial knots in Maroon Perle cotton for the collar and sew on the small gold

heart. Back stitch around the nose, eye and ear in two strands of Black cotton.

STEP TWO

Embroider the stone pathway in stem stitch, using Pale Brown wool.

STEP THREE

Work the blue daisy petals in lazy daisy stitch, using Dark Blue cotton with a French knot centre in Pale Yellow cotton. Stitch the stems and the lazy daisy leaves in Dark Green.

STEP FOUR

For the sunflower petals, work straight stitches in Gold cotton with French knots in Red cotton in the centre. Embroider the stems in stem stitch in Medium Green cotton, then work fly stitches very close together, in the same colour, for the leaves.

STEP FIVE

Work the grass in straight stitch, using Medium Green cotton.

STEP SIX

Work the trunk and branches of the pine tree in chain stitch, using Teal Blue cotton, and the lines on the ground in straight stitches in the same colour.

STEP SEVEN

Work the trunk and branches of the cherry trees in stem stitch, using Lime Green cotton. Embroider the cherries in Red French knots.

STEP EIGHT

Work the trunk and the branches of the apple tree in stem stitch, using Khaki Brown. Embroider the apples in colonial knots, using Maroon cotton.

STEP NINE

Embroider the sun in French knots, using Yellow cotton and the sunbeams in straight stitch in the same colour. Make sure the sun will be facing in the right direction when the bag is finished. Embroider the eyes in French knots in Pale Brick cotton and the mouth in straight stitch in the same colour.

MAKING UP

STEP ONE

Following the pattern, cut the point of the flap on the lining and the embroidered piece.

STEP TWO

Fold the front of the bag, as before, with the completed embroidery on the inside. Pin the sides together, then stitch. Repeat for the lining, leaving an opening on the end of the bag. Place the lining inside the bag with the right sides together. Stitch the bag and the lining together at the flap and the top of the bag, leaving a 7.5 cm (3 in) opening at the top of the bag. Turn the lining and the bag right side out and hand-stitch the opening closed.

STEP THREE

To make the twisted cord, cut 2 m (2¼ yd) of the Cream yarn and twice 2 m (2¼ yd) of the Tan yarn. Put them together, then fold the length in half. Attach one end around a door knob, or something similar, and twist the other end until it is very tight. Fold the twisted threads in half, allowing them to twist back on themselves. Tie a knot in the end with the cut ends, then tie a knot in the other end. Attach the twisted cord to the inside of the bag securely, at the fold, with a few oversew stitches.

STEP FOUR

For the tassel, cut twice 1 m (1⅛ yd) of Tan yarn and 1 m (1⅛ yd) of Cream yarn. Put them together and wind them fifteen times around the cardboard. Tie off the top (Fig. 2). Remove the yarn from the cardboard. Wrap Tan yarn around the tassel 1.5 cm (⅝ in) from the top (Fig. 3). Cut through the yarn at the bottom of the tassel. Blanket stitch around the top of the tassel starting at the wrapping (Fig. 4). Keep working rounds of blanket stitch into the previous row, until you have covered the top, then attach the tassel to the bag.

Bold colours and stitching are a feature

Fig. 2

Fig. 3

Fig. 4

For reasons of space, this design is given at 90%
of actual size. Enlarge it on a photocopier.

SILK BRIDAL BAG

This dainty bridal bag is perfect for the special bride in your life. Created with silk, roses and lace, it will be a lasting memento of her special day.

MATERIALS

35 cm x 110 cm (14 in x 44 in) of ivory dupion silk

3 m (3¼ yd) of 6 mm (¼ in) wide double-faced ribbon, Ivory

50 cm (20 in) of 10 mm (³/₈ in) wide double-faced ribbon, Ivory

75 cm (30 in) of 7 mm (⁵/₁₆ in) wide double-faced ribbon, Ivory

65 cm (26 in) of 15 mm (⁵/₈ in) wide ivory cotton lace

65 cm (26 in) of 15 mm (⁵/₈ in) wide ivory cotton beading

75 cm (30 in) of 7 mm (⁵/₁₆ in) wide silk ribbon, Ivory 1

50 cm (20 in) of 7 mm (⁵/₁₆ in) wide silk ribbon, Green 73

75 cm (30 in) of 4 mm (³/₁₆ in) wide silk ribbon, Green 73

Madeira Embroidery Silk, Green 1708

Waterlilies by Caron, 1 skein of Morning Mist Variegated

Gold cupid charm (I used a Guardian Angel for good luck!)

Gold thread

Chenille needles, size 22

Crewel needles, size 9

Note: See page 6 for the appropriate needles to use with each type of thread or ribbon.

Sewing thread to match the fabric

Water-soluble marker pen

PREPARATION

See the embroidery design below.

STEP ONE

Cut a 35 cm x 60 cm (14 in x 24 in) piece of the silk. Fold the fabric in half lengthwise and mark the halfway point. On this line, mark a point 7 cm (2³/₄ in) in from the raw edge. This is the point where you will begin your embroidery.

STEP TWO

Place the design under the fabric and trace the design with the marker pen. If you are unable to see through the fabric to trace the design, tape the design to a window with the daylight coming through it. Tape the fabric over the top, then trace the design onto the fabric.

STEP THREE

Place the fabric in the hoop, ready to commence the embroidery.

EMBROIDERY

STEP ONE

To make the large folded rose, marked **A** on the design, use the 10 mm (³/₈ in) wide double-faced ribbon. Stitch the rose in place on the design.

STEP TWO

Make the small folded rose, marked **B** on the design, in the same way as the large rose, but using the 7 mm (⁵/₁₆ in) wide double-faced ribbon.

STEP THREE

To make the bud, marked **C** on the design, use the 7 mm (⁵/₁₆ in) wide double-faced ribbon and the method described on page 11. Stitch the leaves on either side of the bud using ribbon stitch and the 7 mm (⁵/₁₆ in) wide Green silk ribbon (Fig. 1).

STEP FOUR

Stitch the silk ribbon buds, marked **D** on the design, using the 7 mm (⁵/₁₆ in)

Embroidery Design

Fig. 1

Nestle the gold charm among the roses

wide Ivory silk ribbon and working two straight stitches, one on top of the other, going in and out of the same holes. Fly stitch around the buds in a single strand of Madeira Silk, then work a second fly stitch, close to the first, making it slightly longer to give a feathery look. Finish with a straight stitch in the middle of the bud, beginning at the base and going down halfway up the bud (Fig. 2).

STEP FIVE

Stitch the leaves, marked **E** on the design, using the 4 mm ($^3/_{16}$ in) wide Green silk ribbon and ribbon stitch.

STEP SIX

Work French knots, marked **F** on the design, in two strands of Waterlilies Morning Mist, scattered throughout the design.

STEP SEVEN

Using the Gold thread, stitch the cupid in the centre of the embroidery.

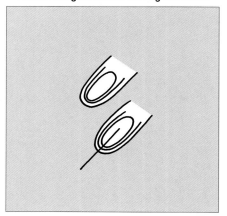

Fig. 2

MAKING UP

STEP ONE

Sew the short ends of the fabric together, with the right sides facing, to form a circle. Fold the fabric in half lengthwise so the seam is on the inside and the back of the embroidery is hidden. Sew the lace along the top edge on the fold line with a very small zigzag stitch. Then sew the beading to the bag with the top edge of the beading 2.5 cm (1 in) from the previously stitched lace edge (Fig. 3).

STEP TWO

Cut two 12 cm ($4^3/_4$ in) circles from the remainder of the silk fabric. Run a gathering thread by machine or by hand along the bottom of the bag, through both thicknesses of fabric. Pull the gathering thread up to match the circumference of the fabric circles. Turn the bag inside out and baste one circle to the bag, then stitch it in place.

STEP THREE

Turn the bag right side out. Turn under a small hem on the second circle of fabric and hand-stitch it in place on the inside of the bag. You should have no seams showing.

STEP FOUR

Cut the 6 mm ($^1/_4$ in) wide ribbon in half. Thread one piece of ribbon through the beading from one side of the bag, then repeat with the other piece of ribbon for the other side. Tie a knot in the ends of the ribbons and pull them up to close the bag.

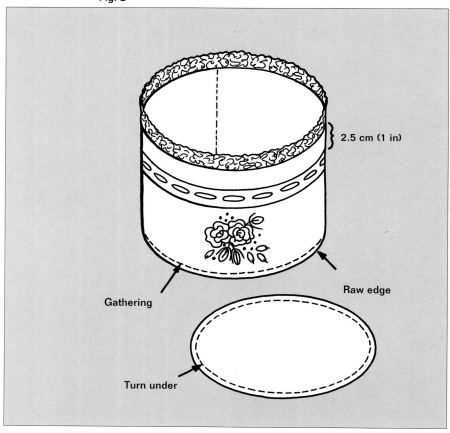

2.5 cm (1 in)

Gathering

Raw edge

Turn under

Fig. 3

SILK RING PILLOW

With the initials of the bride and groom and the little buds with silk ribbons to tie the rings in place, this is a very special pillow for a special day – a keepsake to be treasured forever.

MATERIALS

1 m (1¹/₈ yd) of 115 cm (45 in) wide ivory dupion silk
30 cm x 40 cm (12 in x 16 in) piece of Pellon
Two 4.5 cm (2 in) cherubs
DMC Metallic Thread, Gold 282
Sewing thread to match the ribbon
30 cm (12 in) zipper
Crewel needles, size 9
Chenille needles, size 20
Note: See page 6 for the appropriate needles to use with each type of thread or ribbon.
27 cm (10¹/₂ in) embroidery hoop
3.5 m (4 yd) of 25 mm (1 in) wide double-faced ribbon, Ivory
2.5 m (2³/₄ yd) of 15 mm (⁵/₈ in) wide double-faced ribbon, Ivory
1.5 m (1²/₃ yd) of 10 mm (³/₈ in) wide double-faced ribbon, Ivory
2 m (2¹/₄ yd) of 7 mm (⁵/₁₆ in) wide silk ribbon, Ivory 1
1.4 m (1¹/₂ yd) of 4 mm (³/₁₆ in) wide silk ribbon, Ivory 1
2 m (2¹/₄ yd) of 4 mm (³/₁₆ in) wide silk ribbon, Green 73
Waterlilies by Caron, Morning Mist 100% Silk
Madeira Embroidery Silk, Green 1708
Water-soluble marker pen

PREPARATION

See the embroidery design on the Pull Out Pattern Sheet.

STEP ONE

Cut out the pillow front, as described in the general instructions for assembling a cushion on page 14, making the front measure 30 cm x 40 cm (12 in x 16 in). Cut two pieces for the back: one 15 cm x 30 cm (6 in x 12 in) and one 30 cm x 32 cm (12 in x 12¹/₂ in).

STEP TWO

Fold the fabric in half horizontally then vertically to find the centre. Finger-press the folds.

STEP THREE

Place the embroidery design under the fabric for the front and trace the design with the marker pen. If you are unable to see through the fabric to trace the design, tape the design to a window with the daylight coming through it. Tape the fabric over the top, then trace the design onto the fabric.

Delicate colours and textures combine in this beautiful piece

71

STEP FOUR

Baste the Pellon onto the back of the fabric, then place it in the hoop ready to commence embroidery.

EMBROIDERY

STEP ONE

To make the large rose, marked **A** on the design, fold the 25 mm (1 in) wide double-faced ribbon into a rose. The more folds, the larger the rose. Make four and stitch them to the pillow front.

STEP TWO

Make the medium rose, marked **B** on the design, in the same way, using the 15 mm (⁵/₈ in) wide double-faced ribbon. Make two and stitch them to the pillow front.

STEP THREE

Make the small rose, marked **C** on the design, in the same way, using the 10 mm (³/₈ in) wide double-faced ribbon. Make two and stitch them to the pillow front.

STEP FOUR

Make the large buds, marked **D** on the design, using the 10 mm (³/₈ in) wide double-faced ribbon, as described on page 11. Stitch the buds in place.

STEP FIVE

Work the leaves for the buds, marked **E** on the design, in the Green silk ribbon. Work a ribbon stitch on either side of the bud, starting at the base and going down halfway up the side of the bud (Figs 1 and 2).

STEP SIX

Stitch silk ribbon buds, marked **F** on the design, using the 7 mm (⁵/₁₆ in) wide Ivory silk ribbon. Stitch two straight stitches one on top of the other to form a padded bud. With a single strand of the Green embroidery silk, do a fly stitch around the buds, then work another fly stitch close to the first, but slightly longer than the other. This gives the bud a nice wispy look. Place a straight stitch coming up at the base of the bud and going down in the centre of the bud (Fig. 3).

STEP SEVEN

Stitch the leaves, marked **G** on the design, in ribbon stitch in the Green silk ribbon where they are indicated in the design. Add some lazy daisy stitches around the buds in a single strand of Green embroidery silk.

STEP EIGHT

Sew the cherubs in place, using the Gold thread

STEP NINE

Work French knots, marked **I** on the design, in three strands of the Waterlilies Morning Mist. Scatter them around the design and in bunches around the flowers and cherubs.

STEP TEN

Satin stitch the initials in a single strand of Waterlilies Morning Mist thread. Place a single bud and leaf in the middle of each initial.

MAKING UP

Make up the pillow, following the general instructions for assembling a cushion on page 14.

Fig. 1

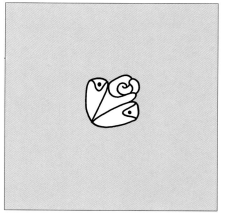

Fig. 2

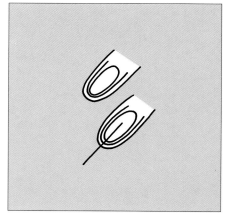

Fig. 3

73

HEART CUSHION

The antique colours and the fabric of this cushion would enhance the decor of any room where a soft muted look is desired.

MATERIALS

1 m (1¹/₈ yd) of 115 cm (45 in) wide seeded cotton damask
40 cm (16 in) square of Pellon
20 cm (8 in) embroidery hoop
35 cm (14 in) zipper
2 g (1 tsp) of silver-lined seed beads
Chenille needles, sizes 18-24
Crewel needle, size 8
Note: See page 6 for the appropriate needles to use with each type of yarn or thread.
DMC Laine Colbert Tapestry Wool: Grey Blue 7295, Pale Plum 7253, Medium-dark Plum 7255, Dark Plum 7266, Old Gold 7494, Yellow Gold 7473, Green 7392, Deep Plum Pink 7210, Very Pale Lavender 7260
Paterna Persian Yarn: Dark Green A600, Medium Pink A925, Pale Pink A935, Medium Green A603
Ordinary sewing thread to match the fabric
40 cm (16 in) cushion insert
Water-soluble marker pen

PREPARATION

See the embroidery design on page 77.

STEP ONE

Cut out the cushion front, following the general instructions for assembling a cushion on page 14, making the front measure 40 cm (16 in) square.

STEP TWO

Fold the fabric for the front in half horizontally then vertically to find the centre. Fingerpress the folds.

STEP THREE

Place the embroidery design under the piece to be embroidered and trace the pattern with the marker pen. If you are unable to see through the fabric to trace the design, tape the design to a window with the daylight coming through it. Tape the fabric over the top, then trace the design onto the fabric.

STEP FOUR

Baste the Pellon to the back of the cushion front piece. Place it in the hoop, ready to commence the embroidery.

EMBROIDERY

STEP ONE

For the Grey Blue flower, marked **A** on the design, work five petals in the following manner. Using the DMC Grey Blue, for each petal, work one long straight stitch in the middle and two short straight stitches on either side of the centre stitch. For the centre, work a French knot in DMC Yellow Gold (Fig. 1). Embroider lazy daisy stitch leaves in Paterna Medium Green.

STEP TWO

For the dark plum roses and buds, marked **B** on the design, work three bullions of approximately four wraps in the DMC Dark Plum. Work scattered

Fig. 1

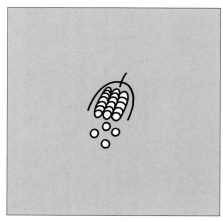

Fig. 2

Fig. 3

French knots in DMC Dark Plum with two straight stitches in the same colour for the buds (Fig. 2). For the leaves, work lazy daisy stitches in Paterna Dark Green; fly stitch around the buds in the same coloured yarn.

STEP THREE

For each deep pink daisy, marked **C** on the design, work five lazy daisy stitch petals in DMC Deep Plum Pink. Work a French knot in the centre of the flower in DMC Old Gold.

STEP FOUR

For the gold flower cluster buds, marked **D** on the design, work two small straight stitches going in and out of the same hole, one on top of the other, for the bud centre in DMC Old Gold. Using DMC Green (split in two), work fly stitches around the buds. Work French knots and lazy daisy stitches for the leaves in the same Green (Fig. 3).

STEP FIVE

For the gold daisies, marked **E** on the design, work a small straight stitch for each of the five petals in DMC Old Gold. For the leaves, work lazy daisy stitches in DMC Green (split in two).

STEP SIX

For the plum rose buds, marked **F** on the design, work a centre bullion of four wraps in DMC Medium-dark Plum. Work two other bullions of six wraps on either side of the centre one in DMC Pale Plum. Work a fly stitch

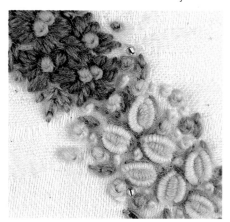

Scatter seed beads for a pretty effect

around the bud (Fig. 4). Work lazy daisy stitch leaves in Paterna Dark Green.

STEP SEVEN

For the medium-to-dark plum blossoms, marked **G** on the design, work lazy daisy stitches grouped together in a cluster in DMC Medium-dark Plum. Work lazy daisy stitch leaves and scattered French knots in DMC Green (split in two) (Fig. 5).

STEP EIGHT

For the mixed-coloured blossoms, marked **H** on the design, work scattered French knots throughout the design in DMC Very Pale Lavender and Pale Plum.

STEP NINE

For the hollyhocks, marked **I** on the design, work blanket stitches in Paterna Medium Pink (Fig. 6). Work the leaves in lazy daisy stitch and the French knots in Paterna Medium Green.

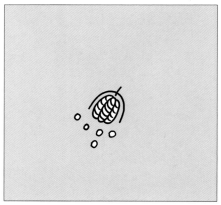

Fig. 4

Fig. 5

STEP TEN

For the pink rose buds, marked **J** on the design, work one bullion of six wraps for the centre in Paterna Medium Pink. Work one bullion of approximately eight wraps on either side of the centre in Paterna Pale Pink. Using DMC Green (split in two), work fly stitches around the buds and lazy daisy stitch leaves (Fig. 7).

STEP ELEVEN

Scatter French knots in Paterna Pale Pink throughout the design. Sew on the seed beads at random so they will pick up the light.

MAKING UP

Make up the cushion following the instructions for assembling a cushion on page 14.

Fig. 6

Fig. 7

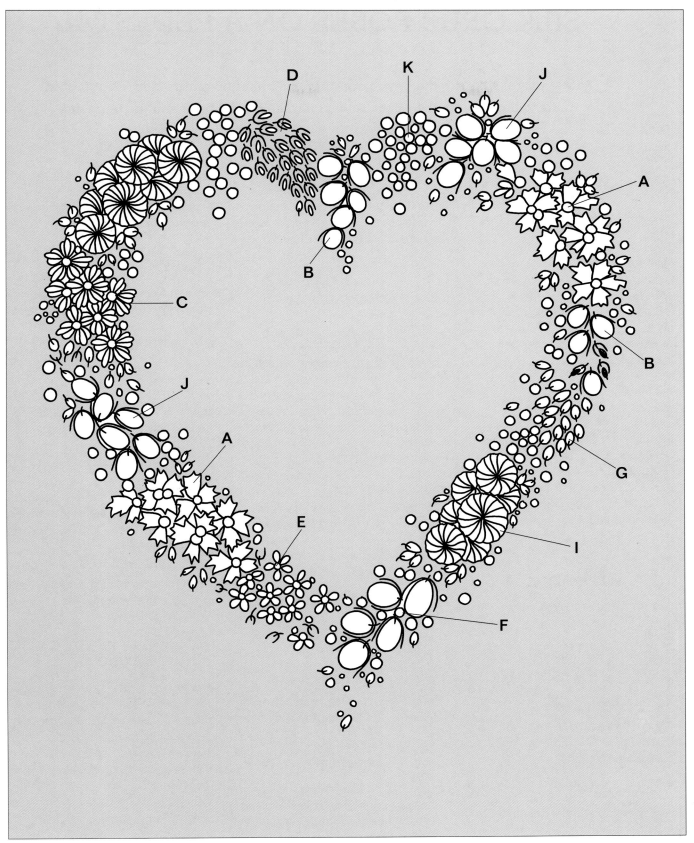

Embroidery Design

SILK GRUB ROSES ON A PEDESTAL

Subtle pastel silks are the key to creating this beautiful embroidery. A soft gold frame will complete the effect, enhancing the gold thread and the pedestal.

MATERIALS

25 cm x 30 cm (10 in x 12 in) of fine silk fabric
25 cm x 30 cm (10 in x 12 in) of cotton organza or Pellon
25 cm x 30 cm (10 in x 12 in) of Pellon
12 cm (4¹/₂ in) embroidery hoop
Crewel needles, size 10
Straw needles, size 9
Fine metallic thread, Gold
Pedestal
Kanagawa Metallic Yarn, Green 7
Waterlilies by Caron, Pistachio Nut
Au Ver a Soie Silk Threads: 1011, 1012, 1813, 1814, 2941, 3011, 3322, 3323, 3332, 4241, 4242, 4621, 4631, 4632, 4633, Cream
Water-soluble marker pen

PREPARATION

See the embroidery design on page 80.

Note: All the silk thread embroidery is worked in a single strand.

STEP ONE

Fold the fabric in half vertically and horizontally to find the centre. Fingerpress the folds.

STEP TWO

Place the embroidery design under the fabric, matching the centres. Mark the top half of the pattern onto the fabric with the marker pen – the pedestal goes on the bottom half.

STEP THREE

Baste the cotton organza or Pellon to the back of the fabric. Place it in the hoop, ready to begin embroidering.

EMBROIDERY

STEP ONE

For the grub rose centre, using the straw needle, work two bullions of five wraps each. Next, work four bullions of seven wraps around the centre. On the outside of the rose, work six bullions of six wraps each.
• For rose 1: work the centre in 4633, the middle in 4632 and the outside in 3332
• For rose 2: work the centre in 4621, the middle in 1012 and the outside in 1011
• For rose 3: work the centre in 4242, the middle in 4241 and the outside in Cream
• For rose 4: work the centre in 3323, the middle in 3322 and the outside in 3332
• For rose 5: work the centre in 3011, the middle in 2941 and the outside in 1011
• For rose 6: work the centre in 4633, the middle in 4632 and the outside in 4631

STEP TWO

For the rose buds work two bullions of five wraps each, side by side, using the straw needle. Stitch a fly stitch around each bud, using a single strand of 1814.

STEP THREE

Work the leaves in lazy daisy stitch in a single strand of 1814.

STEP FOUR

Embroider the fern in fly stitch in a single strand of 1813 or the Kanagawa thread, alternating the two different threads. Stitch a straight stitch for the tip of the fern in the same colours.

STEP FIVE

For the highlights, embroider straight stitches in Gold thread, using the picture as a guide.

STEP SIX

Scatter French knots in two strands of Pistachio Nut quite densely around the centre of the design and to the outside of it.

STEP SEVEN

Stitch on the pedestal using the Gold thread and invisible stitches.

MAKING UP

Remove the embroidery from the hoop and take out the basting threads. I always place an additional piece of Pellon behind my pictures before they are framed, as it gives the work more loft. Frame your picture or have it done professionally.

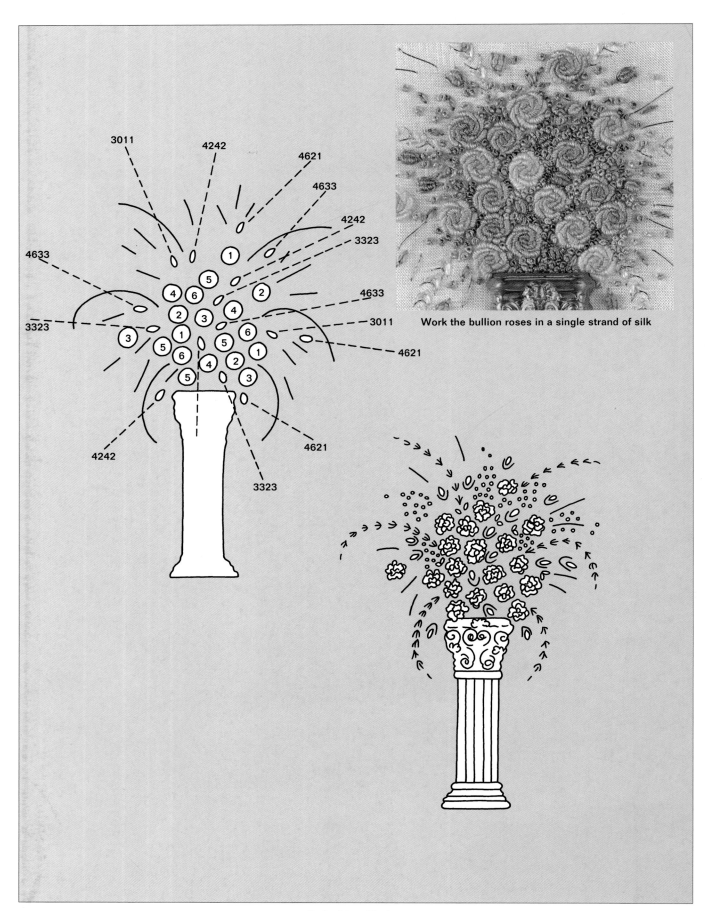

3011

4242

4621

4633

4242

3323

4633

3323

4633

3011

4621

4242

4621

3323

Work the bullion roses in a single strand of silk

Embroidery Design